IRISH FERRIES
An Ambitious Voyage

Miles Cowsill • Justin Merrigan

Ferry
Publications

Published by:
Ferry Publications, PO Box 33, Ramsey, Isle of Man IM99 4LP
Tel: +44 (0) 1624 898445   Fax: +44 (0) 1624 898449
E-mail: ferrypubs@manx.net   Website: www.ferrypubs.co.uk

Irishferries.Com

1

The *Isle of Inishmore* alongside at Dublin's berth 51A having completed overhaul relief duties on the Holyhead service in January 2013. (Derry Walsh)

Publisher's Notes

This publication, which chronicles the history of Irish Ferries and its parent company Irish Continental Group plc (and the constituent companies B&I Line and Irish Continental Line whose enterprises they embody), is the sole unaided work of its authors and publisher.

Whilst every care has been taken in assembling the information that it contains, Irish Ferries cannot accept responsibility for any errors of fact, any unintended breaches of copyright, any oversights, omissions or erroneous attributions, or any opinions that may be expressed therein.

Irish Ferries compliments the authors and publisher on their comprehensive approach to the subject and commends their work to readers, researchers, marine historians and those involved in the world of transport, shipping and tourism.

Acknowledgements

The authors are extremely grateful to all those who have assisted with this book. We are indebted for all the support and involvement from Irish Ferries, especially Eamonn Rothwell, Tony Kelly and Garry O'Dea and particular thanks to Don Moore, Irish Ferries Archivist, for his guidance and provision of material.

The publishers are also grateful to the following for their assistance with photographs and information for the book: Alex Brown, Brian Cleare, Derry Walsh, Don Hall, Don Smith/Pictureships, Gordon Hislip, Ian Collard, John Cave/Holyhead Maritime Museum, John Hendy, John McKenna, Kenneth Whyte, Lynne Keating, Maritime Photographic, Mike Pryce, Paddy Cahill, Ronald Roberts and Svein Torske.

Contents

Produced and designed by Ferry Publications trading as Lily Publications Ltd
PO Box 33, Ramsey, Isle of Man, British Isles, IM99 4LP
Tel: +44 (0) 1624 898446   Fax: +44 (0) 1624 898449
www.ferrypubs.co.uk   E-Mail: info@lilypublications.co.uk

Printed and bound by Printo Trento, Italy
© Ferry Publications 2013
First Published: August 2013

Foreword

By virtue of our status as an island nation, ships and shipping have always had a special role to play in the life of the Irish nation and always will. With over 90% of the country's trade moving by sea, the importance of the ferry industry cannot be overstated.

As an open economy – one that relies heavily on exporting goods to overseas markets, in bringing in the products and raw materials that our society needs to function, and in providing access for the many thousands of tourists who come to holiday in Ireland every year – the contribution being made by the roll-on, roll-off passenger car ferry industry is especially important. Indeed, it is the export sector that will underpin Ireland's future economic growth. Indeed, it is the export sector that will underpin Ireland's future economic growth. Irish Ferries will continue to play a critical role given its current carryings of over €9 billion of exports on an annual basis.

At Irish Ferries, we are extremely proud of the contribution we have made, and continue to make, in serving the needs of the Irish people over generations. We are proud of the investments we have made and of the position of leadership that we enjoy within the sector as reflected in the acquisition of our modern fleet and in the improvements we have wrought in the area of customer services generally – all of which was made possible through the generous support of our shareholders.

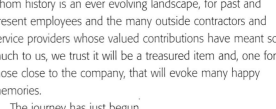

Eamonn Rothwell (Irish Ferries)

In both an Irish and international context, the story of Irish Ferries is surely one worthy of being recorded. At one level, it is the story of two eminent shipping companies, B&I Line and Irish Continental Line, whose separate operations were brought together in the early 1990s to form the new enterprise known today as Irish Ferries.

In their separate ways, both of these fine companies enjoyed a distinguished history dating back to the early 1800s, one serving routes between Ireland and Britain and the other between Ireland and mainland Europe. At various stages, they were in private and Government ownership but now are part of a public company quoted on the Irish and UK stock exchanges. This allows everyone the opportunity to own part of the business and share in its future.

As this publication comprehensively records, in bringing these two fine companies together under the Irish Ferries flag, a new, modern, forward-looking company was created – one whose focus was, and still remains, firmly fixed on cost leadership and customer service within an organisation that never compromises safety.

Central to this development and the growth that the company has experienced has been the commitment made by our shareholders. Being part of a larger, publicly quoted shipping enterprise, Irish Ferries has benefited enormously by being free to chart its own course without dependence on any State funding. This has led to Irish Ferries having one of the most modern fleet of ships in the world, custom built for each of its routes and culminating in the building of the world's largest ferry in 2001, an especially proud moment. And indeed, being voted Best Ferry Company in Ireland's annual travel trade awards on fifteen occasions in the last eighteen years is a great credit to all of our staff and suppliers, ashore and afloat.

In this publication, authors and publisher alike have told our story in a most comprehensive and entertaining way. In doing so, they have justly recognised the immense contribution that management, staff and crew make in helping to satisfy the expectations that our freight customers and passengers have of us.

We commend all whose inputs have made this publication possible. We salute the writers, contributors, photographers and designers whose collective contributions have captured the richness of our history and committed it to paper in an entertaining and readable format that surely will be enjoyed by all.

For the public and those interested in shipping and transport matters generally, for academics and archivists for whom history is an ever evolving landscape, for past and present employees and the many outside contractors and service providers whose valued contributions have meant so much to us, we trust it will be a treasured item and, one for those close to the company, that will evoke many happy memories.

The journey has just begun.

Enjoy!

Eamonn Rothwell

Eamonn Rothwell
CEO, Irish Continental Group plc, August 2013

The *Isle of Inishmore* on her delivery voyage to Ireland from her Dutch builders in 1997. (FotoFlite)

Introduction

As is true today, the island of Ireland has long been very reliant on its sea routes for trade and commerce. Every year, Irish Ferries alone transports over 1.5 million passengers and 350,000 cars, in addition to more than 180,000 lorries on routes from Dublin and Rosslare to Wales and to France.

Through its acquisition of the former state-owned B&I Line in 1992, Irish Ferries has a long and proud heritage, the company's roots going way back to the early 1800s and the formation of the City of Dublin Steam Packet Company, the City of Cork Steam Packet Company and the British and Irish Steam Packet Company.

Ireland's first car ferry services to and from France were introduced in 1968. Normandy Ferries' *Leopard* sailed from Le Havre to inaugurate a link with Rosslare – a service which in its first year of operation was very successful, conveying some 15,000 passengers and 4,000 cars. In 1971 Normandy Ferries withdrew from the service and former partners Irish Shipping began the search for suitable ships to continue the route. In 1973 the link was restored by its subsidiary, Irish Continental Line, with the ferry *Saint Patrick*, and over the years the service blossomed. The 1984 demise of its parent company, Irish Shipping, could have spelt doom for the successful Irish Continental Line, but the business survived and entered a new phase in 1987 under the control of the Irish Continental Group plc.

Just 5 years later, in 1992, the Irish Continental Group took over B&I Line including its Dublin-Holyhead and Rosslare-Pembroke Dock services – a very positive decision which not only put the privately-owned pioneering company in direct competition with key rivals Sealink Stena Line, P&O Irish Sea and Brittany Ferries but which, as this book illustrates, also proved a boon for tourists and freight businesses alike.

Irish Ferries, the new owners of B&I Line, moved quickly to improve operations and services. Replacement tonnage and newbuilds firmly established the company as a leading operator from Ireland to both the UK and to France. This included an entry into the fast ferry world in 1999 with the building of the catamaran *Jonathan Swift* in Australia with a creative new design of accommodation which has stood the test of time. In 2001, in its most ambitious investment yet, Irish Ferries placed an order with Aker Finnyards in Finland for a giant 12-deck ship with capacity for 2,000 passengers and crew, 1,342 cars and 240 trucks. When subsequently introduced into service between Dublin and Holyhead, the *Ulysses* was the world's largest car ferry in terms of vehicle capacity and is still the largest ferry operating between Ireland and the UK.

Also impressive for its size is the *Isle of Inishmore*, the largest and most luxurious ferry serving Ireland's Southern Corridor of sea routes to and from Ireland, specifically between Rosslare and Pembroke Dock – a service which has grown since it was established by B&I in 1980. In 2007, in a further move to improve the quality of operations between Ireland and France, Irish Ferries purchased the *Kronsprins Harald* from the Norwegian company Color Line. Renamed *Oscar Wilde* after an extensive refit, she entered service on the Roscoff and Cherbourg routes.

city centre, allows easy access for all traffic leaving or arriving at the ferryport.

As for the ships, all three cruiseferries – the *Ulysses, Isle of Inishmore* and *Oscar Wilde*, together with the Dublin-Holyhead fastcraft *Jonathan Swift* – offer excellent service and facilities. And despite the difficulties created by the global economic downturn from 2008, the company has remained profitable throughout a very testing trading period – a testament to the foresight and quality of Irish Ferries' management, which has radically but shrewdly streamlined operations in order to remain very competitive with its Irish Sea rivals.

The *Ulysses* inward bound to Holyhead from Dublin off The Skerries. (Ronald Roberts)

Extensive recent and ongoing road improvements in the UK to Holyhead and Pembroke Dock have allowed these ports to improve and expand their own operations. The much-enhanced A55 from Chester to Holyhead enables traffic to reach Holyhead from the M6 in less than 2 hours. On the Southern Corridor, work continues on developing better links to the A477 from the M4/A40, the final stages due for completion by 2018. In Ireland, road connections from Rosslare have also improved radically, in particular to Dublin, where the new tunnel from the port to the M50, bypassing the

The history of both B&I and Irish Ferries is a fascinating story, and the authors are grateful to the directors for allowing it to be told in this book. As for the long-term future, the company is well placed to continue to play a leading role in Ireland's enduring and prized shipping industry.

Miles Cowsill and Justin Merrigan
August 2013

Chapter one

Fresh Thinking

Before he settled into the ferry business, Irish Continental Group's Chief Executive Officer Eamonn Rothwell spent his early working life in financial journalism, followed by a spell with the Irish Tourist Board and then on to investment management with Allied Irish Investment Bank, specialising in the equity markets of the US, Japan, UK and Europe.

He set up the equity desk for the emerging NCB Stockbrokers, working closely with Dermot Desmond. In 1987 Eamonn arranged the purchase, and 1988 stock market flotation of, Irish Continental Group (ICG), joining the Board as a non-executive director. He advised ICG on the purchase of B&I, which took over two years to execute, and it was on its completion that he was appointed Group CEO.

It was around the time of ICG's stock market flotation in 1988 that Eamonn approached Garry O'Dea, now the Group's Finance Director, to join him. Dublin-born Garry had completed a commerce degree before training as a chartered accountant with the international professional services firm KPMG, where he qualified in 1979. In 1981 he joined Irish Cement Ltd at its CRH plc headquarters – the biggest plc in Ireland at the time. On progressing to ICG, Garry immediately set about modernising the Group's finance department.

For many years B&I had been struggling, in terms of both customer service and financial performance. ICG saw an opportunity to reposition the company and was particularly attracted by the potential of its business on the short routes between Ireland and the UK. When B&I (as it became) applied for emergency aid in 1990, negotiations were opened by ICG to purchase the company from the State. By late 1991, after the second round of negotiations, and with the highest bid, the deal was done. Even though it would be a big challenge, the objective was to keep the existing routes open and to invest shrewdly and as necessary. The purchase was closed on a Friday and on the following Monday Eamonn took command of ICG as CEO.

It soon became apparent that B&I was floundering because of its policy of putting greater focus on its own staff than on customers and prospects, and in addition operating costs were too high. The latter was due in part to the size of its ships – smaller than those of competitors such as Stena Line and P&O, with a consequent higher unit cost per lane metre. In 1992 roughly 70% of the Republic of Ireland's ro-ro freight imports and exports were going through ports in Northern Ireland. ICG's thinking was that this figure should be closer to 50%, given the density of population, the level of integration and the structure of sea connections. The belief was that with the right lane metres sailing at the right times ICG could retrieve a lot of business – hence a new determination to build bigger ships, especially for the Central Corridor, even though it would be no easy task.

During the next 12 years (1992-2004), a huge effort was made to streamline the company's cost base and refocus on customers. While there were successful

was to survive against international competition. The voluntary uncapped severance programme of 2005, which aroused a lot of negative media coverage was broadly welcomed by staff who understood that things had to change – as evidenced by the 93% acceptance level of the offer. The uncapped nature of the offer (with some staff receiving up to €.25m) and the ease of getting alternative jobs in an Irish economy which was then running at virtually full employment undoubtedly

Eamonn Rothwell (Irish Ferries)

milestones along the way, the apparent intransigence of the unions, deeply embedded since prior Government ownership of the company, allied with successive national wage agreements lead to erosion of competiveness and the creation of a serious disadvantage relative to competitors. Many of these competitors were international companies which were immune to any excesses caused by the Celtic Tiger economy that was Ireland in the first decade of the century.

Continuous change management, customer service training and all too frequent strike disruptions were all in a day's work during this twelve year period.

Eventually, the writing was on the wall that something fundamental had to change if the company

helped to smooth the transition which took place.

Almost 10 years on, Eamonn still cites that volatile and confrontational period as a critical time in the survival and development of ICG, from understanding the true value of the short-sea slots to purchasing B&I – a brand then virtually worthless – and investing heavily in a new and much more profitable way of doing business. Without his long-term vision, the company could well have gone down then with no survivors.

Much of the financial success of Irish Continental Group was attributed to the *Pride of Bilbao* (then called the *Olympia*). The company's initial interest in her was as potential for its French operations and using one ship instead of two, but she was too expensive. The situation

Garry O'Dea (Irish Ferries)

changed when the currency crisis hit and her Swedish owners went into receivership. Irish Ferries enquired again – not for use on French operations but much more as a long-term investment for the company. Speedy negotiations with banks and liquidators ensued and in less than 6 weeks the vessel was bought, having been renamed the *Pride of Bilbao* and already committed to a charter to P&O Portsmouth for an initial 3 years with renewal options. The long-term significance of this investment in the ship is described further on in the book, but suffice it to say here that in addition to helping to fund the *Isle of Innisfree* it provided the company with a regular income and was excellent security in dealings with banks.

Initially B&I was run separately from Irish Ferries but when it was eventually decided to merge the brands, the Irish Ferries management took over and most of the B&I senior management left. In its first couple of years this new set-up concentrated on cost cutting to make the brand viable. The *Niels Klim* (renamed the *Isle of Innisfree*) was chartered around December 1991 just prior to the takeover and later moved from the Rosslare to the Dublin route; subsequently, the *Isle of Inishmore* transferred to Rosslare.

By this time Eamonn Rothwell was leading the change and focusing on economies of scale, utilising larger ships with similar crew numbers to move much more freight. The newbuild *Isle of Innisfree (II)* was delivered in 1995, followed soon after by the *Isle of*

Inishmore (II) and then by the *Jonathan Swift* and the *Ulysses* – and the freight market was improving.

By replacing tonnage and providing a far better service than at any time in the past, the company is today not only stable but enjoys high standing in the international ferries arena. However, as Eamonn Rothwell understands only too well, there are difficulties inherent in further expansion. Unlike airlines, which can add new routes to their services with relative ease, Irish Ferries cannot easily add new routes so organic growth is crucial. Acquisitions are often difficult because of limited opportunities driven by poor trading of certain routes whilst better performing companies often demand unrealistic conditions of sale. And in the process of replacing old tonnage with new purpose-built ships, the company has been very focused on the need to make a healthy return on each such investment in the passionate belief that, long term, this is beneficial to customers too.

In transforming the fortunes of ICG, Eamonn Rothwell emphasises that the people involved were the key to its achievement. Those who played a significant role included the late Alex Mullin (former Operations Director), the late Captain Coleman Raferty (former Shipping Director), Frank Carey (former Marketing Director), and John Reilly, Tony Kelly, Garry O'Dea, Eddie Keane, Brendan McCarthy and Alf McGrath. The Board was generally very supportive throughout the difficult period of Irish Ferries' history led initially by Tom Toner and then by John McGuckian.

The loss of duty-free in 1999 was a big blow but a problem which all ferry companies and airlines had to accept and overcome. In fighting off the airlines during the last 10 years (the likes of Ryanair and Aer Lingus) Irish Ferries has targeted its key markets with campaigns which emphasise the comfort, ease, relaxation and attentive customer service which passengers travelling with Irish Ferries can expect, and of course emphasising (at least for many travellers) the biggest benefit of all – being able to travel with their car and all the baggage it can carry and enjoy the freedom to tour as the fancy takes them.

Of course, airlines and ferry companies each have their particular niches in the market. However, in the last few years there have been signs that Irish Ferries is beating off the airlines, with more families returning to the option of going by sea. Ferries have the extra benefit of carrying freight too, but it's passengers who are now (in 2013) far more important to Irish Ferries, passenger share of revenue running at 70% compared with 55% at the peak of the economic cycle in 2007, when the freight

Eamonn Rothwell pictured with Lord Sterling, Chairman P&O Group plc (1995). (Irish Ferries)

share grew to 45%.

Financially, the advent of outsourcing (which started on the French route in 2004 and was extended to Irish Sea routes in 2005) also helped the company to remain stable throughout a downturn in the global economy. Outsourcing leaves the company in full control of its own ships (owning the fleet and the brand, dictating schedules and so on) but puts recruitment, employment and management of the crew, and day-to-day operations, in the hands of independent companies. So all high-level strategic and management decisions remain with Irish Ferries but staff recruitment and management are the responsibility of the appointed suppliers.

The decision to move forward as a business in this way proved its wisdom with the advent of the global financial crash in 2008. With such a competitive cost base, Irish Ferries was in good shape to withstand the impact despite the reduction in freight traffic and revenue. Others in the industry weren't so well prepared.

In March 2007, in response to the company's largest institutional investor looking for a "liquidity event" (and given the difficulty of rolling out the ICG model into new markets), Eamonn Rothwell and the senior management team approached the Board with a view to making an offer to all shareholders. After protracted negotiations the Board agreed to recommend an offer at a premium of 25% on the then share price. The shareholders were not entirely surprised by this management buyout offer to take ICG off the Stock Market – but some were shocked by the fact that such a move was started only after the revitalisation of the company, with shares up to an extremely healthy level. Quoted in *The Sunday Times*,

Eamonn said that he would not be comfortable availing himself of weak markets to try to buy the stock: "For me it's not about money, it's about quality of life." However, it was also seen that Eamonn was determined to hold on to the business. He is noted as saying, "I have invested a lot of sweat and equity into turning this business around." Few would argue or doubt that ICG is Eamonn's baby and that he not only steers the company but will continue to protect it from predators.

Since 2007 the management has been through negotiations likened by one Dublin analyst to a spectacularly high-stakes poker game. On the announcement of the offer some new investors, including event-driven hedge funds, bought shares in the company and rejected the management-led offer, which lapsed. Subsequently, these shareholdings, with the help of the company, were all placed back with the market at substantial discounts. Today ICG is still listed on the stock market, Eamonn being the largest shareholder with just under 17% of the company.

Eamonn Rothwell has proven over and over that he is a force to be reckoned with. His combination of rare natural talents and insights enables him to mix good business sense with an ability to not only see how the markets are moving but predicting what *will* work, what *won't* and when the time is right to make a change. He is fiercely loyal but shuns the limelight, leaving the company's success to speak for itself. Whatever happens in the coming years, it's clear that with Eamonn at the helm Irish Ferries will remain the stable and respected company that it is today.

The Commercial Challenges

By the mid 1960s operations on the English Channel were ahead of those on the Irish Sea. Double-deck linkspans were in use in Dover, and the first drive-on drive-off ferries came on stream in 1964 between Southampton and Cherbourg, at a time when cars and freight on the Irish Sea were still being loaded on and off by crane. The Irish Sea's first drive through roll-on roll-off ferry was British Rail's *Antrim Princess*, working the Stranraer-Larne service in 1967, and B&I introduced its own drive-on drive-off ferry *Munster* in 1968. But it was not until 1995, with the *Isle of Innisfree*, that double-deck linkspans were put to work on the Irish Sea.

Come the early 1970s B+I was a large business, certainly by Irish standards. A multitude of sub-businesses included not only a ferry division but also road haulage, groupage and container divisions and deep-sea agencies, as well as many of the traditional aspects of a steam packet company. As technology slowly began to influence the lift-on lift-off business, and ro-ro ferries emerged as serious players in the market, B+I led the way in utilising mechanised handling systems, welcoming freight revenue as a valuable complement to passenger traffic. By the mid-70s B+I had a strong market presence – a major brand representing real competition for the likes of Sealink. But although it was an exciting time, problems began to develop – symptoms of the company's need to manage all aspects of its ships and terminals.

The industrial unrest of the 70s and early 80s led to a particularly hard time for B+I. Relationships with customers were good, enabling the company to stay ahead of the market, but strikes and failed negotiations were problems which rocked everybody's boat. It wasn't until Mininster of Labour Bertie Ahern (later to become Taoiseach – Prime Minister) stood up before Parliament in 1987 and made his "There is no more room for concessions or for brinkmanship…" speech that the tide began to change, albeit very slowly, towards privatisation in 1992.

Following the early years of reorganising and planning after the ICG (Irish Continental Group) purchased B&I, the company took full advantage of the realisation that with change came the opportunity for growth. A direct result was the building of the *Isle of Innisfree* for the Holyhead route in 1995. With a greater capacity and a more efficient operation than previous ships, the benefits of the investment were immediate; almost overnight, freight traffic opted to go through Dublin on the *Isle of Innisfree* rather than take the longer option via Belfast or Larne. "We knew we had a serious success with our first newbuild," said Tony Kelly, Freight Manager at that time, "and it led pretty quickly to the decision to go again and build the *Isle of Inishmore.*" Indeed, the *Isle of Innisfree* was a lesson in not only creating a good product and applying affordable pricing but also demonstrated the company's serious and total commitment to the Irish cause.

In early 1997 Tony Kelly was appointed a director of the company and succeeded his predecessor, Frank Carey, taking on responsibility for both the passenger and freight sides of the business. The *Isle of Inishmore* was delivered and commenced trading from Dublin, the *Isle of Innisfree* moving south to the Rosslare–Pembroke service. Within two years the routes had been transformed, the market reacting favourably and business growing. By this time the Irish economy was growing too, enabling Irish Ferries' freight business to compensate for the more complex passenger operations.

With the *Isle of Innisfree* and *Isle of Inishmore* serving the Pembroke and Holyhead routes, the next step was to introduce a fastcraft service. This expansion was driven purely by a desire to remain viable against the competing ferry services and to uphold the good name of Irish Ferries as the fast, efficient, local ferry operator.

After market consultations and financial considerations, the *Jonathan Swift* was built for the company in 1999 by Austal Ships in Australia. In a bold move Irish Ferries decided against a traditional seating design in favour of a more convivial configuration – a reversed/mixed seating arrangement more in keeping with the concept of a relaxed, informal holiday atmosphere and experience, and allowing passengers the freedom to walk about. A philosophy of "let's make it really enjoyable, let's make it different" was further reflected in the recruitment of crew – a shift in emphasis from the traditional ferry market selection process, with youthfulness and enthusiasm complementing experience. Passenger reaction was favourable and instant, furthering the cause of getting the new-style look and service off the ground. As for adding speed to the Irish Ferries travel experience, the *Jonathan Swift* lived up to its name, crossing the sea between the centre of Dublin and Holyhead in just 1 hour 49 minutes.

By this time a combination of good business sense and the courage of the company's convictions ensured that the development of the Irish Ferries brand was proceeding as planned. In 1998 Irish Ferries had added the *Normandy* to the fleet, specifically for the continental corridor route. Although there were real limitations in terms of the wisdom of heavy investment on the Ireland-

Tony Kelly (Irish Ferries)

France routes, and main competitor Brittany Ferries was enjoying subsidies that Irish Ferries wasn't, it was felt that a continued presence on these services was desirable. The initial charter and purchase of the *Normandy* had its limitations, due to the age of the vessel and the need to invest in its non-public areas, but the business grew nevertheless. Investing in four ships over as many years was an ambitious but successful move.

With business expanding it soon became clear that the *Isle of Inishmore* would go the same way as the *Isle of Innisfree* by being a victim of her own success, even though, at that time, she was the largest ferry in north-west Europe. Running as she was to full freight capacity on most nights of the week, it was tempting to see only good times ahead. By mid 1999 the options on the way forward were clear: to keep going with the *Isle of Inishmore* on Dublin-Holyhead services (which would immediately limit growth in a strong economic environment); to add a second vessel to run in tandem (which would be very inefficient); or to build an even bigger ship. In the belief that a quantum leap in capacity would pay handsome dividends, the third option won the day – a decision which was arrived at quickly, given that in terms of hierarchy Irish Ferries is comparatively small and enjoys the benefit of being able to act swiftly when it is commercially advantageous to do so. Hence, remarkably, the whole project to conceive, design, construct and deliver the new ship – the *Ulysses* – took less than 14 months from start to finish.

Driven by Eammon Rothwell's vision to achieve that quantum leap in capacity, the design concept called for an extra deck, internal ramps and other innovative features which together presented a vehicle deck capacity virtually double that of the *Isle of Inishmore* – in all, over four kilometres of vehicle space, making it at that time the biggest ferry in the world. It was quite an achievement for a relatively small Irish company, the giant *Ulysses* duly entering service in early 2001.

But, out of the blue and completely unpredictably, it was at about this time that Ireland succumbed to an outbreak of foot-and-mouth disease – a massive blow, effectively closing the door on the country's tourism business, regular announcements in the UK press discouraging visitors. Despite this, the Irish economy was still growing and freight traffic fared better than passenger business. Better still, the *Ulysses* was an instant success, impressive for her size, onboard style and tremendous sea-keeping abilities – a testament to the company's foresight in investing in design and propulsion which allowed her to dock in even the roughest weather.

From 2008, as the massive downturn in the Irish economy was taking effect (particularly in the construction sector, which had been one of the biggest drivers of the preceding boom), the impact on the Irish ferry markets was very significant. Whilst many of Irish Ferries' competitors had continued to increase capacity as the economy peaked, others had invested in additional tonnage even after the decline had begun. The timing of the company's own investment in new tonnage was fortuitous in enjoying a decade of the so-called Celtic Tiger economy and achieving a balance sheet capable of sustaining Irish Ferries through the severely stormy waters of 2008 and beyond. Had the investment and consequent reorganisation not occurred in 2004/2006, the outcome

might have been far different.

A constant and crucial factor in steering the company through waters calm or otherwise is understanding the ferry markets – knowing what's happening within them and where they are likely to go, and being as proactive as possible, rather than falling foul of delaying vital decisions to the point that it's too late to change or influence the outcome. Irish Ferries is also driven by the belief that it can hold its own against the bigger international players, rather than by market share alone, sustaining business by remaining both competitive and attractive to customers, and never being afraid to admit if it gets things wrong – but never shouting from the rooftops about its successes. The company ethos is one of care, caution and honesty, applied consistently and in equal measures to both maintain a steady course and ensure the business's ongoing development.

Another important factor in the equation is that unlike its competitors, Irish Ferries is bound by the status of its parent company, Irish Continental Group, which trades as a plc (public limited company). This requires ICG to declare specific details of its performance in interim and final statements and annual reports, and there are clear Stock Exchange rules by which it must abide. None of Irish Ferries' competitors has any such obligation to put information into the public domain, and as a relatively small international company it is not in Irish Ferries' nature to court attention or raise its corporate voice, even when its performance tables are there for everyone to see. However, the last 10 years have produced solid results, the directors having personal stakes in the business and caring deeply about its fortunes in every sense. Of course, from an investor's point of view, a business is only as successful as its most recent results.

Irish Ferries' approaches to the key market segments

With the building of the *Ulysses* Irish Ferries considered a number of logo designs for the ship. The view above, and illustrations on page 15, show some of the designs which were considered for the new ship and the rest of the fleet. (Irish Ferries)

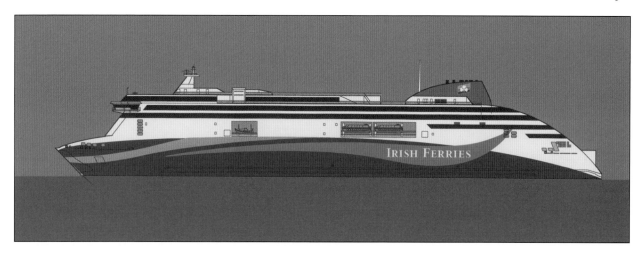

(passenger and freight) differ from each other quite radically. Whilst marketing, distribution and delivery of passenger products and services are increasingly influenced by the latest requirements of consumer legislation, a much more confidential business-to-business relationship exists between the company and its freight customers.

Within the last decade or so a major hurdle faced by all ferry companies has been the competition posed by airlines. By around 1997 it became increasingly difficult to attract ferry passengers as airlines initiated more regional routes, and the ready availability of affordable long-haul flights put exotic breaks within easier reach at the expense of, for example, the traditional two-week family holiday in Ireland, two days of which would typically be consumed by driving.

In the early 2000s Irish Ferries became the first ferry company to tackle the airlines head on, with marketing campaigns focused on declining airline standards. Other ferry companies soon followed. It was an effective ploy, people recognising what they already knew and felt

themselves – the inconvenience of airport hassle, the lack of space and security, and other grievances. And after the 9/11 terrorist attacks in particular, the perception of airline travel altered radically from glamorous to restrictive. By comparison, ferry travel was undergoing a quiet revolution and although in reality standards generally had been vastly improved, there were ingrained memories and impressions of how things used to be. Hence ferry companies exploited the advantages of the freedom of ferry travel (in particular the ability to take your own car and all the baggage it could carry) and the restrictions and costs inherent in going by air.

In spring 2010 came a significant but totally unexpected turning point in favour of ferry travel – Iceland's infamous volcanic ash cloud, which grounded aircraft far and wide and left many airline travellers stranded. A large number of them turned to ferries and made their way home by sea. Although short-lived, the drama created a new awareness of just how far modern ferries and the experience of ferry travel had come; for example, the ease with which it was possible to return to

London by train from the Irish Ferries terminal at Holyhead. And for Irish Ferries the eruption had a knock-on effect, heralding a year or so of increased business.

DOING THE BUSINESS

As for any company in any field of business, Irish Ferries' continued success is dependent on providing the products and services which customers and prospects are looking for, and at prices perceived as representing good (if not outstanding) value for money – on the face of it, a standard and universal proposition.

But there are very significant and obvious differences between ferry travel and, for example, the daily consumables we all take for granted. Analysis over many years has shown that even those ferry travellers classed as regulars tend to sail only once or twice a year, and 'serious' ferry users just slightly more often than this. So in terms of being in the minds of customers and prospects at the opportune moment, and fighting alongside rival operators and airlines, timing is crucial. In the leisure travel market taking on the airlines is particularly challenging, given that it's now possible to fly to just about anywhere.

"What Volcano" billboard in Dublin (2010). (Irish Ferries)

In overall terms the majority of visitors and holidaymakers choosing Ireland as their preferred regular destination are British, and the Irish Tourist Board has to work hard to promote and maintain this market. In such a highly competitive business there is no room for complacency, as Irish Ferries is only too well aware. There was a time when Ireland lost its lustre to familiarity and

Blooms Bar - *Ulysses* **(Maritime Photographic)**

was perceived as too expensive and not offering value for money.

France is also a source of visitors to Ireland, although this is something of a niche market – a very small percentage of total visitor numbers. The French tend to have a slightly spiritual view of the island, favouring the west of the country, whereas British visitors are more drawn to the cities. But French visitors represent a valuable, though modest, asset for Irish Ferries. Germany too provides an important stream of Ireland's tourism income, many visitors travelling with their cars either from France or via Britain.

Holidays and tourism aside, much of the Irish Ferries market is to do with catering for people who travel for business and leisure, the latter including a significant number visiting Ireland to see friends and relatives. Constantly reminding such travellers of the benefits of using the services of Irish Ferries is all part of the company's ongoing marketing mix and activity.

BRAND IDENTITY

Any brand worth its salt is based on strong and durable core values – and implicit within the very name

Irish Ferries is the promise that nobody knows Ireland as well as the company does, and nobody is better equipped to point visitors in the direction of wherever they want to go or whatever they want to see when they leave the ship. And the Irish also enjoy an enviable and global reputation for warmth, hospitality and good humour – which is all very well, but in the commercial world it has to stack up against harsh economic considerations such as price, service and value for money.

Some people see ferry travel merely as a commodity – a means to an end – and plump for the cheapest option. Others choose on the basis of where the ferry goes from and where it arrives. Departure, arrival and sailing times can also be a big factor, particularly if reaching the final destination on leaving the ferry involves a long drive, and vice versa on the return journey. And how the ferry company is perceived in terms of quality, service and reliability also impacts on bookings.

Understanding and accepting that no one company can appeal to everyone all of the time, Irish Ferries targets specific market segments, especially those where traditionally it has a strong customer base and where little threat is posed by airlines. The era of online bookings

Café Lafayette - *Oscar Wilde* **(Maritime Photographic)**

means that today sales can be won or lost on the strength of the quality, clarity, speed and ease of navigation of the website, which is a crucial business tool: it has to inform immediately, without ambiguity, and allow customers to purchase easily, quickly and securely.

The same applies to the mobile phone revolution, which similarly has made booking so much easier, more convenient and secure, and Irish Ferries was amongst the first ferry operators to have a version of its website accessible to smart phones. Irish Ferries also led the way in providing live online reservations long before many of the bigger players had progressed from a message/request booking system. Irish Ferries' current (2013) reservations system is the product of a three-year development and implementation project, and the majority of bookings are facilitated in this way. But, typically of Irish Ferries, those customers who still prefer to book by phone are well catered for too, enabling them to speak directly to someone who has immediate answers to questions and queries.

The final factor in Irish Ferries' commercial equation is yield management – the science of maximising yield and profits by being flexible with pricing, in line with daily demand and what is happening in the market place. Prices for early booking are always lower and, with the aid of technology, matching or beating what competitors are charging at any particular time is possible whenever it makes commercial sense to do so but without compromising the core values of the Irish Ferries brand. Best of all, it's customers who benefit.

FREIGHT BUSINESS

Freight is a crucial component of the Irish Ferries marketing mix and the company is committed to maintaining and developing strong commercial relationships with its many customers in Ireland, Britain and across mainland Europe. Unlike the seasonal peaks and troughs of passenger traffic, freight provides an income for 52 weeks of the year in the shape of Ireland's imports and exports, and commercial agreements can make sound financial sense. In recent years this part of the business has also embraced the latest technology to remain both cost-effective and highly competitive.

THE SHAPE OF THINGS TO COME

So how does Irish Ferries see the future of ferry travel? Inevitably, ever-smarter technology will play a big role in transactions, very likely to the point of customers purchasing tickets on their mobiles and arriving at port with minimal check-in demands – "a seamless use of clever technology."

Another aspect of changing times is the ongoing search for new fuel options with which to power ships present and future, as demanded not only by regulations

Irish Ferries wins Best Ferry Company at annual Irish Travel Awards 2007 : left to right – Dermot Merrigan, Michael McGlynn, Declan Mescall, Marie McCarthy, Ann Pye, Tony Kelly, Vincent McMahon, Bernadette Green, Nick Mottram, Daragh O'Reilly. (Irish Ferries)

Café Lafayette and Kilronan Motorist's Club - _Isle of Inishmore_ (Maritime Photographic)

governing engine emissions and sea pollution but also by unsustainable costs. As for the ferry travel experience itself, comfort, speed and onboard services such as accommodation, entertainment, leisure, shopping, catering and communication will continue to drive design and innovation, in line with passengers' ever-growing expectations.

In 2013, at two separate award ceremonies, the Irish travel trade voted Irish Ferries Best Ferry Company – an annual accolade which rewards performance, commitment and service in an increasingly competitive industry. Tony Kelly is quick to point out that without people who are willing to push the commercial boundaries every day, Irish Ferries could all too easily find itself playing second fiddle to its competitors.

"The success of the company throughout the last 30 years has been dependent on many terrific individuals – too many to mention by name – who have all played, and continue to play, their part in the development of the company's relationships with customers and suppliers. This has included people who have worked long and hard in our many markets, and others who have brought solutions to tricky and complex problems whilst never losing the desire to succeed and improve the performance of the business."

Clearly, the future and continued success of Irish Ferries is in the experienced and expert hands of its own very capable people.

Chapter three

Sea
Change

One of the great strengths of the company's fleet directors has been to openly embrace necessary change. Five years after initiating the transition to becoming a public limited company, Irish Ferries and B&I merged and it was decided to pool resources and utilise the companies' own ships for annual dry dock relief. As the conditions and terms for both companies differed, and working systems changed, making longer-term accommodation acceptable was important. The *Niels Klim* demonstrated just how good accommodation could be, helping personnel to accept that change could benefit the company, and over the course of two to three years investment in new branding, training and uniforms significantly improved the service and ethos of Irish Ferries.

When the Irish Continental Group was in the process of taking over B&I in 1991 it was recognised that there were challenges ahead, as was true for many other ferry operators at that time. With the company spending modestly and looking to the future and possible building programmes, the *Munster* charter came up for renewal. As potential purchasers ICG advised B&I to cancel the charter to prevent the renewal from rolling over, resulting in the *Munster* being re-delivered around April/May of that year – John Reilly's (retired Operations Director) first job with B&I. By 1992 the *Niels Klim*, renamed the *Isle of Innisfree*, had replaced the *Munster* and although slow at 17.5 knots she had great capacity and was an interim step for building up the Dublin-Holyhead route, helping to create the opportunity for the company to move towards building bigger ships.

When the *Pride of Bilbao* was bought in 1993 she was seen as a leap forward for the company – a new ferry built to Baltic standards and generating regular income from a reputable charter to P&O for its Spanish market. This income took Irish Ferries through to 1995, when its first new-build, the *Isle of Innisfree (II)*, was put in place. Although the charter income decreased over the years as the ship aged, option periods were renewed by mutual agreement until the time when only the *Pride of Bilbao* was trading the western service. Captain Eddie Keane (retired Fleet Director) believes that by investing in the initial purchase price of the *Pride of Bilbao*, the ship was key in changing the status of the company.

A new-build negotiation with Samsung in 1993-94 which failed at the last minute suddenly left B&I without the ship they had hoped for, and the company decided to look at what other shipyards were producing. Van der Gieesen-de Noord was chosen to create a new vessel based on an adapted *Norbay/Norbank* design and, once contracts were signed, the yard worked closely with Irish Ferries throughout the build. The design was lengthened by 30 metres, accommodation added to the front of the vessel and, with space for 1500 passengers and 1800 metres of lane capacity, the *Isle of Innisfree (II)* was huge. There was a great sense of achievement in seeing the ship go from the planning stage to completion – the "arrival of the future for Irish Ferries".

Although by the mid 1990s the company was aware of the development of high-speed ferries, and was interested in them up to a point, the key matters of

8 or 9 with specifications led again to Van der Gieesen, the yard contracted to build the *Isle of Inishmore (II)* – at that time Irish Ferries' biggest ship, strong but simple, very well constructed and boasting a quick turnaround, higher standards of accommodation and space for 2,200 passengers. She was delivered in 1997 but, as with the *Isle of Innisfree (II)*, soon after she entered service she too was working to full capacity and the company was again in the unhappy position of turning away business.

The open-door policy within Irish Ferries soon encouraged an exchange of ideas, and plans were

The *Isle of Innisfree* glides through the English Channel en route to Dublin on her delivery voyage in 1995. (FotoFlite)

operational costs, fuel economy and other expenses led to the fundamental decision that it made better financial sense to concentrate on building bigger, more conventional ferries.

In 1995 the *Isle of Innisfree (II)* gave a taste of a new world and boosted the company with the introduction of new livery, branding, uniforms and upgraded training. However, the ship achieved full capacity almost immediately and it was obvious that a bigger ship was required. Researching a dozen shipyards and approaching

conceived for yet another new ship. The most important issue, especially at Dublin given the width of the River Liffey, was manoeuvrability – a problem the company had already addressed successfully in the design and construction of the *Isle of Inishmore (II)* – and with specifications duly drawn up the contract to build the new ship, the *Ulysses*, went to Aker Finnyards in mid 1999. By March 2001 she was in service. Aker proved a pleasure to deal with and delivered an outstanding product. Fitting out the ship was done at great expense and to a much

SH·FERRIES

An impressive view of the *Isle of Innisfree* prior to her launch in 1995 at Van der Giessen de Noord. (Ferry Publications Library)

The *Isle of Innisfree* seen shortly after her launch in fitting-out prior to her delivery to the company in May 1995. (Ferry Publications Library)

higher standard than that of any previous vessel in the fleet, utilising quality products and materials and superior design expertise to create what was then the world's largest and most reliable car ferry. The ship's construction was overseen by an excellent Irish Ferries team led by John Reilly, Captain Eddie Keane and Brian Larkin and comprising deck engineer Derek Corrigan, chief engineer Jim Corrigan and electrical engineer Liam Magnier.

During this period the company also benefited from another major external charter of the *Isle of Innisfree*. First chartered to P&O for the Cherbourg service in 2002 as the *Pride of Cherbourg*, her work on this route was short lived and she was sub-chartered to Stena Line for six months on the Baltic service. Following this, Stena then subchartered her to New Zealand on the inter-island service, where she continues to trade, successfully maintaining a welcome and regular long-term source of income for Irish Ferries.

An artist's impression of the self-service restaurant on board the *Isle of Innisfree*. (Irish Ferries)

An artist's impression of the main bar on board the *Isle of Innisfree*. (Irish Ferries)

The company decided to embrace fast ferry technology in the late 90's having monitored closely the developments in this market throughout Europe in the previous few years. As the new millennium approached, Irish Ferries responded to customers growing expectations of a fastcraft service. The major factors in designing the new vessel were comfort and build quality, the latter steering the contract to the Australian yard of Austal. Delivery of the very appropriately-named *Jonathan Swift* was due in 1999, and although a significant investment at the time, 14 years on her sleek lines continue to impress and, more importantly, she has proven her reliability and ability to maintain a popular high-speed service.

From the early concept stages Irish Ferries realised, the *Jonathan Swift* needed a USP (unique selling proposition) to offer passengers something special in the way of high-speed sea travel. This was admirably achieved with the combination of an original new seating arrangement, onboard entertainment and Austal's impressive glass atrium. For Irish Ferries there were other very significant and lucrative spin-off benefits too. The fact that many car and foot passengers soon preferred to travel on this high-speed service but also to gradually phase out night sailings given that the *Jonathan Swift* ran round the clock, completing four round trips a day in

With the success of the *Isle of Innisfree* Irish Ferries contracted Van der Giessen de Noord to build their second Ro-Pax vessel. This view shows the *Isle of Inishmore* prior to her launch. (Ferry Publications Library)

The *Isle of Inishmore* is manoeuvred to her fitting-out berth after her launch in 1996. (Ferry Publications Library)

The *Isle of Inishmore* pictured inward bound from Holyhead as the Australian-built *Jonathan Swift* makes her way out of Dublin port during 1998. (Irish Ferries)

summer.

In 2007, when the *Oscar Wilde* replaced the *Normandy* on the French services to Cherbourg and Roscoff, the impressive and highly competitive new Irish Ferries fleet was complete. The need to replace the *Normandy* had been vital, and the acquisition of the *Oscar Wilde* from Color Line as she became available introduced a much higher quality of accommodation and increased freight space – the ideal ship in the company's desire to expand and improve its operations in this market.

By learning from other companies in the early days, especially those in the Baltic market renowned for their high standards of service, training and efficient operation,

The Normandy replaced the *St. Killian II* and Saint Patrick II on the continental services in 1998. (FotoFlite)

A computer generated impression of the *Ulysses*. (Irish Ferries)

The *Ulysses* under construction in Rauma, Finland, 2000, prior to being floated out. (Irish Ferries)

Eamonn Rothwell with John Reilly, Operations Director, Irish Ferries with *Ulysses* under construction in the background. (Irish Ferries)

Irish Ferries has boldly embraced change. Although much admired, not all aspects of the Baltic operations (notably conference, spa and cruise services) were deemed suitable for Irish Ferries' continental market, but following the French in terms of much more emphasis on family-orientated catering has reaped its own rewards.

Today's ferry passengers the world over are ever more demanding in terms of quality and diversity of onboard services, and Irish Ferries' introduction of Club Class in particular has made the travel experience much more refined.

On a warm spring-like day the *Ulysses* arrives at Dublin for the first time from Finland on 4th March 2001. (Irish Ferries)

In 2001 the *Isle of Inishmore* was transferred to the Rosslare-Pembroke Dock route to boost capacity on the Southern Corridor operations. (FotoFlite)

31

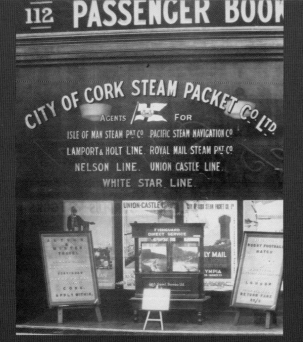

Chapter four

Anchored in time

Trade links between Dublin Bay and Holyhead have existed since the Romans arrived on the Welsh Isle of Anglesey, but it was during the reign of Elizabeth I that the importance of the link was cemented. The Queen's postal communications with her Lord Lieutenant in Ireland crossed the Irish Sea to Dublin from Liverpool until, in the period 1573-76, a route was established via Holyhead, although the line's development was extremely slow.

In August 1818 the Irish mail packet terminal moved from Dublin's Pigeon House to a new harbour at Howth, north of the city, reducing the passage time between Dublin and Holyhead. Initially Howth proved to be a far easier port to access than Dublin (which suffered from the presence of a sandbar), but it was soon realised that the new harbour too had its access problems come winter's frequent easterly gales. On the opposite (south) side of Dublin Bay, ongoing construction work was in progress to build a new Asylum Harbour at Dun Laoghaire (Dunleary). Although it was intended as a refuge for sailing ships awaiting entry into Dublin, some of the new Post Office paddle steamers began to use the East Pier berth available there in 1827.

It came as little surprise when Howth was closed as a packet station on 22nd January 1834 and replaced by Dun Laoghaire (at this time known as Kingstown). The London & Birmingham Railway chose to send mail for Ireland through Liverpool rather than Holyhead, and on to Dublin by steamer via Kingstown, and in 1836 the railway invited the City of Dublin Steam Packet Company to tender for the contract. Consequently, the London mail was sent via Liverpool and the Chester mail through Holyhead.

The City of Dublin Steam Packet Company was formed in 1823 under the name of Charles Wye Williams and Co. The ambitious Williams, one of the unheralded pioneers of steam navigation, and his co-manager Mr Francis Carleton, also set their sights on establishing a transatlantic steam service. This opened on 5th July 1838, the steamer *Royal William* sailing from Liverpool to New York – the first powered westbound crossing between the two ports. But the enterprise was unsuccessful and Francis Carleton and the directors of the then Peninsular Steam Company formed the Peninsular and Oriental Steam Navigation Company – more familiar today as P&O.

The last paddle steamers ordered by the Admiralty for the Holyhead mail service were built in 1847 at a cost of £39,000 each. The *Banshee, Caradoc, Llewellyn* and *St Columba* were fast ships and, given favourable conditions, could make the crossing in just over 4 hours.

The Post Office soon realised that operating ships was far from simple and invited tenders from private companies to take over the service. Two were received, from the Chester & Holyhead Railway and the City of Dublin Steam Packet Company.

THE RAILWAY ERA

The coming of the railways greatly improved communications between London and Dublin. In 1848 the Admiralty decided that the mail between the two cities should go via Holyhead rather than Liverpool. In doing so they also took over the sea crossing to Kingstown using the four packet ships. On 1st August 1848 the mails were placed on London Euston's *Irish Mail* train at 21.45 and reached Holyhead (after transfer to road transport at Bangor) at 06.43. It was two years later that the final section of the London-Holyhead railway line, across the Menai Strait to Holyhead, opened.

From 1st January 1850 the City of Dublin Steam Packet Company (CDSPC) was awarded the contract to run both the day and night mail service from Holyhead – much to the chagrin of the Chester & Holyhead Railway, which had invested heavily in new steamers and infrastructure in expectation of winning the contract, based on the fact that had it done so the mail would remain in the company's care for the entire journey between London and Dublin. Believing the contract to be rightfully theirs, the bitterly disappointed railway company used its ships to carry passengers to Kingstown and cargo and cattle to Dublin's North Wall without the lucrative rewards of the mail contract.

The victors of the contract battle, the City of Dublin Steam Packet Company, purchased the *Llewellyn* and the *St Columba* from the Admiralty and added two of its own ships, the *Eblana* and the *Prince Arthur*, to offer a Kingstown-Holyhead service with an average passage time of 4 to 5 hours. An Act of Parliament enabled the company to raise the capital to construct four magnificent steam vessels to maintain the Holyhead service. The order was placed in 1859, when the new Carlisle Pier was opened at Kingstown, and the vessels were named after the four provinces of Ireland: the *Connaught* (I), *Leinster* (I), *Munster* (I) and *Ulster* (I). Their speed of 17 knots was in line with the mail contract's demand of a reduced passage time of 3 hours 45 minutes, a penalty of 34/- (£1.70) to be imposed for every minute late.

In matters of shipbuilding Charles Wye Williams was always to the fore and at the ripe old age of 80 still took a keen interest in the construction of the new steamers, journeying up to London to witness the casting of the cylinders of the *Leinster* at Messrs. Ravenhill, Salkeld & Co. By the time of his death in April 1866, the CDSPC was a formidable company, the finest of steamers running a model mail and passenger service. In 1883 a new contract for the mail service was won by the Chester & Holyhead Railway's successor, the London & North Western Railway, but uproar in the House of Commons by Irish politicians saw it reinstated to the CDSPC.

One-little known but fascinating fact is that these mail boats, and their successors (the paddle steamer *Ireland* of 1885 and the next four *Provinces* of 1896–97) carried the time every day to Kingstown. This was in the form of a chronometer from the Greenwich Observatory, closely guarded on its journey from Greenwich to Euston Station. Here it was handed to the guard of the *Irish Mail* service for the run to Holyhead. Once there it was passed to the safe keeping of the ship's Master. On arrival at Kingstown, the chronometer was checked again by a representative of the Harbour Master in a small observatory located behind the reservoir next to the Royal Marine Hotel. It was then dispatched to Westland Row where it was collected by a Dublin Port official whose duty it was to see that the metal ball at the Ballast Office near O'Connell Bridge dropped at exactly midday, signalling 'Urbi et Orbi'. In an age without radio, this was the 'official' time. In reality, due to the longitudinal difference between Dublin and Greenwich, it was actually 25 minutes after midday, a new law rectifying the situation in 1916.

While the CDSPC was establishing itself at Kingstown, it also began sailings between Dublin/Belfast and London in conjunction with the British & Irish Steam Packet Co. The latter was formed out of a meeting of well-known Dublin traders at the Commercial Buildings in Dame Street on 27th July 1836. On 24th October, Articles of Agreement were concluded between the investors, who included Arthur Guinness, James Ferrier (Transatlantic Steam Ship Company), Richard Williams and James Jameson. One of the company's first directors was Francis Carleton, who was also a board member of the CDSPC.

NEW SHIPS

The British & Irish Steam Packet Company's first ships were the wooden paddle steamers the *Devonshire*, the *Shannon* and the *City of Limerick*, and by 29th December 1836 the company was advertising weekly services between Dublin and London, calling at Plymouth. The company soon chartered three more vessels – the *Nottingham*, the *Mermaid* and the *Royal William* – and, in 1842, the *Duke of Cornwall*, sailing from Dublin's North Wall to London, alternating with CDSPC vessels on Wednesdays and Saturdays and calling at Falmouth and Plymouth. The *Duke of Cornwall* was the last wooden paddle steamer built for the B&ISPC, the company becoming one of the first to invest in propeller-driven ships, in 1845 announcing an order for two vessels – the *Rose* and the *Shamrock* – for the Dublin to London route. In 1850 the *Foyle* was added to the fleet and in 1852 and 1853 came the *Lady Eglinton* (the first B&ISPC steamer with a *Lady* name) and the chartered *Nile* respectively.

In 1897 the CDSPC was awarded an additional 21 years to its contract with the Post Office and duly chose the Cammell Laird shipyard at Birkenhead to replace the *Provinces* with new vessels of the same names. Each cost £95,000 and grossed 2,646 tons. They were twin-screw vessels, 115 metres long and powered by two 8-cylinder steam engines which produced a speed of 24 knots. The onboard sorting office was manned by members of the Dublin Post Office.

An incident at Kingstown in 1908 is notable for its similarity to two separate stand-offs a generation later. Having moved its Irish passenger terminal from Kingstown to Dublin's North Wall in 1864, the London & North Western Railway returned to the south side of Dublin Bay in 1908 with its four *Kingdoms* – the *Anglia*, *Cambria*, *Hibernia* and *Scotia*. This prompted the CDSPC to take the railway company to court in an attempt to protect its territory. The case was lost on the grounds that as the LNWR's predecessor, the Chester & Holyhead Railway, had operated to Kingstown in the last century there was no reason why the railway could not do so again. The relationship between the two companies deteriorated to the extent that something of a battle broke out over available slots at the Carlisle Pier. On 2nd April 1908 the Harbour Master at Kingstown was compelled to write to the Master of the *Munster* (II) ordering him to "forthwith and immediately remove your vessel from her present moorings to the east side of the Carlisle Pier so as to leave the west side clear for the incoming day mail boat and in case of your refusal or neglect to forthwith obey this order I will at once have you proceeded against for the full penalty of £10 imposed by the 22nd Sec of the 6 & 7 Wm. IV cap. 117." The mail boat to which the Harbour Master referred would have been one of the *Munster*'s sisters, and the

order to move would have been necessary to avoid a clash with the next arriving railway steamer.

FIRST WORLD WAR

With trade continually increasing, two major and historic events changed the fortunes of the CDSPC: the division of Ireland and, even more dramatically for the company, the First World War. In 1915 the *Connaught* (II) was commandeered by the War Office and put into service as a troop carrier. The three other *Province* ships continued to operate between Kingstown and Holyhead. On 3rd March 1917, in the English Channel, the *Connaught* was hit by a torpedo and three lives were lost. The three remaining ships had for the most part escaped any involvement with U-boats in the Irish Sea until late in the war. In March and April 1918 the *Ulster* (II) was missed by torpedoes and again in April both the *Munster* and the *Leinster* (II) sighted U-boat periscopes but avoided attack.

But on 10th October 1918, just 32 days before the war ended, the worst fears of all were realised. A little before 09.00, under the command of Captain William Birch, the *Leinster* left Kingstown for Holyhead with 687 passengers, including 30 post office sorters working onboard, plus 70 crew (amongst whom was the great grandfather of one of the authors of this book). An hour into the *Leinster*'s passage, well beyond the Kish Lightship, a torpedo was launched by U-boat *UB-123*. It just missed the *Leinster* but a second torpedo struck the ship in the area of the sorting room, killing all but one of the workers inside. The third torpedo struck amidships in the engine room, causing devastating damage, and the ship began to sink. Passengers and crew, including Seaman John Merrigan (who survived), found themselves struggling in rough seas, and by the time rescue boats arrived 501 had died.

Following the war, the CDSPC could not recover financially from the loss of its ships. With just two vessels left with which to carry the mail and, after political events in Ireland, the absence of a large body of Irish MPs at Westminster to lobby on its behalf, the City of Dublin Steam Packet Company was in no position to bid for the new mail contract. Having carried the mails for 70 years, the company relinquished the contract to its bitter rival the London & North Western Railway. On 27th November 1920, the *Munster* and the *Ulster* sailed with mail for the last time from Holyhead and Kingstown respectively. On the following day the LNWR's *Anglia* sailed with the mails and the two remaining *Provinces* were laid up in the Welsh port pending sale.

Four years passed before they were sold and they left under tow for (ironically) Germany and the breaker's yard. Meanwhile, the company's extensive workshops on Salt Island (Holyhead), the former government dockyards and the timber Mail Pier all fell into disuse. In 1924 the City of Dublin Steam Packet Company passed into the annals of history, and 11 years later many of the workshops and the pier were removed.

CORK SERVICES

As services were developing out of Dublin and Kingstown, so too were crossings in the south of Ireland, from Cork to Bristol, Milford Haven and Glasgow. The St George Steam Packet Company, founded in 1821, grew to considerable size and by the mid-1830s not only had a network of Irish trade crossings but was also heavily involved in deep-sea activities. In October 1843 the company was reorganised, its southern coastal trade passing to the newly-formed Cork Steamship Company.

In 1850 the City of Dublin Steam Packet Company began running to Waterford in retaliation for the Cork company infringing on its trades. In so doing, they went into direct competition with the Waterford Steamship Company, one of whose directors was also a director of the Cork Steamship Company. The Waterford Steamship Company was further challenged by the CDSPC extending its opposition to Cork in conjunction with the British and Irish Steam Packet Company. In response, both the Cork and Waterford companies commenced a weekly service between Britain and the south-east of Ireland – two ships a week between Liverpool and Belfast, and a daily service between Liverpool and Dublin.

And so it continued, the CDSPC offering to carry traffic for Cork and Dublin merchants for free for a period of 3 months. The comeback to this was the threat by the Cork company to place two steamers on the Holyhead and Dublin routes in conjunction with the Chester & Holyhead Railway! A settlement was finally reached in 1851 when the CDSPC transferred its Liverpool-Belfast run to the City of Cork Steamship Company. Three years later the Cork company withdrew from Belfast in return for the Belfast Steamship Company's withdrawal from the Cork-Liverpool service.

With the Cork company's growth continuing, in July 1871 it again reorganised. The Cork Steamship Company concentrated on the deep-sea trade while the home trade came under the banner of the City of Cork Steam Packet Company. The latter's ships retained the black-topped white funnel of the old company and the first

ship ordered under the new concern was the *Upupa*. On 20th October 1881 she rescued 17 survivors from the steamer *Clan Macduff* which had foundered in a strong Irish Sea gale. In January 1903 she herself succumbed to a storm, sinking off the Ballycotton Lightship in a gale while on passage from Cardiff to Cork.

Many vessels came and went but those for which the City of Cork Steam Packet Company became so well known bore the name *Innisfallen*, after Innisfallen Island on Lough Leane, near Killarney. It is believed that here, between the 12th and 15th centuries, the monks of Innisfallen Abbey wrote a chronicle of the medieval history of Ireland containing more than 2,500 entries spanning the years 433-1450 AD.

The first *Innisfallen* was built in 1896. At just under 83 metres long, she was a handsome two-funnelled ship with a displacement of 598 tonnes. In 1906 the Welsh terminal for the Cork line moved from Milford Haven to Fishguard with the opening there of a new port for the Fishguard & Rosslare Railways & Harbours Company – a joint venture of the Great Western Railway and Ireland's Great Southern Railway. By 1914 the City of Cork SPC was operating three each-way sailings a week on the Fishguard run, two each way a week on the Liverpool run, a weekly service to and from Bristol, a weekly round trip from Cork to Plymouth, Southampton and London, and similarly from Cork to Newport and Cardiff, and inward to the Irish port with coal and general cargo.

Of the City of Cork Steam Packet Company's fleet of eight ships, all but two were lost during the Great War. The *Innisfallen,* on passage from Liverpool to Cork, went down some 16 miles off the Kish Lightship after being torpedoed by *UB-64* on 23rd May 1918. This left the company in almost as much difficulty as the City of Dublin Steam Packet Company and, just 2 months after the loss of the *Innisfallen,* an offer for the City of Cork Steam Packet Company from the Royal Mail Steam Packet Company – owners of Coast Lines – was accepted.

Chapter five

Coast Lines
1919-1965

As has been described, such was the level of tonnage losses by the end of the Great War that the City of Dublin Steam Packet Company and the City of Cork Steam Packet Company were in no position to offer a level of service even remotely resembling that of the pre-war period.

However, a tide of consolidation was already underway. In 1917 the British & Irish Steam Packet Company joined the Coast Lines group when the latter purchased Furness Withy & Company's shareholding in the Dublin business. Coast Lines itself was formed by the merging of three companies in 1913, and was known initially by their joint names: Powell, Bacon and Hough Lines. The name Coast Lines Ltd was adopted in April 1917 when the company was taken over by Lord Kylsant's Royal Mail Steam Packet Company.

Coast Lines went on to acquire a controlling interest in a large number of coastal shipping companies, eventually numbering about 20. Among the most important in its lifetime were **British and Irish Steam Packet Company Ltd** (acquired 1917), **City of Cork Steam Packet Company Ltd** (1918), **Tedcastle McCormick** (1919), **City of Dublin Steam Packet Company** (1919), **Belfast Steamship Company Ltd** (1919), **Burns & Laird Lines** (acquired separately as **Laird Line** in 1918 and **G & J Burns** in 1920, merging in 1922), **Tyne Tees Steam Shipping Company Ltd** (1943) and **North of Scotland, Orkney & Shetland Shipping Company** (1961).

Geographically the company's activities spanned the whole of the British and Irish seaboard and extended to the Scottish and Channel Islands. One pleasing aspect of the expansion of Coast Lines was that the individual shipping companies continued to trade under their own names.

The City of Dublin Steam Packet Company's Dublin-Liverpool service, as well as the service to Manchester in which the company enjoyed a shareholding, passed to the British and Irish Steam Packet Company. Along with the transfer came four ships, each name prefixed by *Lady* – the *Lady Louth* of 1906, the *Lady Wicklow* of 1895, the *Lady Carlow* of 1898 and the *Lady Kerry* of 1897. With trade favourable it was decided to revive the passenger connection between Dublin and Liverpool, and in 1920 the route was expanded by 4 ships – the *Lady Martin* of 1914, the new *Lady Kildare*, the *Lady Tennant* of 1904 and the *Lady Meath* of 1906. At the same time the *Lady Louth* was transferred to the City of Cork SPCo and renamed *Bandon*. A brighter and more distinctive image was also unveiled, the B&I ships now carrying a black-topped green funnel.

The ships brought the Dublin-Liverpool service to a level where new-build passenger/cargo ships were appropriate. The new steamers came from the Ardrossan Dockyard Company in 1923 and 1924. The *Lady Louth* and the *Lady Limerick* were the first British & Irish SPCo's purpose-built ships for the Liverpool run and it was very much on these two, plus the *Lady Longford*, that the company developed its core crossing with nightly sailings in each direction. The impact of these ships was immense but as they were often supplemented by fleet mates, it came as no surprise

and the *Kenmare*. The former was to remain a Cork ship for only 2 years before being transferred to the British & Irish SPCo in Dublin. In her place, alongside the *Kenmare*, came the *Lady Killiney*, taking the name of her predecessor.

Long-awaited new passenger tonnage was also destined for the City of Cork SPCo. The *Innisfallen* (II) was delivered in June 1930, taking up service to Fishguard. She was fitted with diesel propulsion and at the time was the only motor passenger vessel running to West Wales, and proved very popular with Fishguard passengers. The ship came from the Belfast yard of

Built in 1893 as the *Magic* for the Belfast Steamship Co, this handsome ship was transferred to the City of Cork SP Co in 1925 as the *Killarney*. She remained with the Cork company until 1930, being replaced by the motorship *Innisfallen*. Coast Lines converted the *Killarney* into a "cruising yacht" sailing from Liverpool to Scotland, which she operated until 1939 when war started. After war service, the ship was laid up until sale to Epirotiki Lines in 1947. As the *Adrias* she foundered on Falconera Island, Crete on 6th October 1951. (John Hendy Collection)

when moves were made to introduce larger tonnage. The Belfast Steamship Company's *Graphic*, *Heroic* and the *Patriotic* were released from their Liverpool duties by new ships and were accordingly transferred to the British & Irish SPCo. The *Lady Longford* stood down on the morning of 7th July 1929 and was transferred to the City of Cork SPCo for service between Cork and Fishguard. The *Lady Limerick* went to Burns and Laird Lines as the *Lairdscastle* in April 1930 and was followed in June by the *Lady Louth*, renamed *Lairdsburn*. Both ships settled well into their new surroundings, taking up the overnight crossings between Glasgow and Belfast.

In 1921 two new steamers entered service on the Cork-Liverpool passenger/cargo service – the *Ardmore*

Harland & Wolff and was finished with a grey hull and two black-topped white funnels but, thankfully, the grey hull was later repainted black! On this new ship's entry into service, the Cork-Liverpool vessel *Kenmare* became the relief Cork-Fishguard ship.

Meanwhile, in 1920, the British & Irish SPCo had established a cartage and motor haulage department in Dublin to replace the company's horsedrawn services for handling the goods carried by its steamers. In 1924 the company bought a fleet of six Albion lorries and by 1930 had a fleet of 30 modern vehicles, including a Maudsley motor omnibus. Dublin's prize horse fleet (which between 1924 and 1942 won at least one prize in the annual RDS Spring Show) was maintained despite the

LIVERPOOL – THE GATEWAY TO IRELAND
BELFAST – DUBLIN

John Hendy collection

advance of the motor vehicle. The company's 78 horses were all known by name, while those in Cork were leased. When petrol became scarce during the 'The Emergency' (as the war years were known in Ireland), more horses were used. The last horse, Smokey, retired in 1973.

After the dissolution of the Royal Mail Group in 1931, Coast Lines became independent under the chairmanship of Sir Alfred Read, who had previously been a director. Interestingly, in 1936 the Irish Government was offered a controlling interest in the British & Irish SPCo (or 'the B&I Line' as it had become popularly known) but they declined, the company remaining with Coast Lines. It was a decision that would soon be regretted. Although an Irish company, in reality the British and Irish SPCo remained under British control.

At the end of 1936 the British & Irish SPCo was placed into voluntary liquidation, emerging on 1st January 1937 as the British & Irish Steam Packet Company (1936) Ltd and acquiring all the Irish interests of the Coast Lines group. This included the City of Cork SPCo, bringing it under the B&I Line banner. Sir Alfred Read emerged as Chairman and Managing Director and the bulk of the shares were taken up by Coast Lines. Sir Alfred was also appointed trustee, with control over the assets of the old British & Irish SPCo, the City of Cork

SPCo and Michael Murphy Ltd, a company in which B&I acquired a controlling interest in September 1926. The bracketed suffix '1936' was dropped from the company's title in 1938. Funnel colours across the B&I fleet became green with a white stripe below a black top, the white embracing the City of Cork SPCo.

In November 1937 the twin-screw motor vessel *Leinster* (III) was delivered at Harland and Wolff in Belfast, followed in March 1938 by her sister, the *Munster* (III). Two new cargo ships were also delivered to the company – the *Kilkenny* (from the Liffey Dockyard) and the *Dundalk*, which was built by Ardrossan Dockyard in Scotland.

Back in Cork on 11th July 1938 it fell to the *Innisfallen* to take home the last British soldiers based at Cork Harbour on Spike Island. The *Irish Times* reported:

*"Amid the booming of guns the last British troops stationed at Spike Island in Cork Harbour this evening handed over custody of the island and the adjoining fortifications to the troops of Eire.
"Spike Island has had a long and interesting history, and for more than 150 years the British flag has flown over it as one of the main defence works on the southern coast. For years Spike was a penal settlement and was continued as such down to the truce of 1921. Today was the seventeenth*

anniversary of the truce. "For the ceremony of taking over the fortifications the Government of Eire sent out a number of invitations, the guests including Ministers, members of the Dáil and Senate, and leaders of the old Irish Republican Army. A decorated train brought the guests from Dublin to Cobh, and a tender carried them to Spike Island, where about 300 Irish troops had already landed under Major Maher. Only a small party of British troops remained, and Captain O'Halloran, who was in charge, handed over the forts to Major Maher on behalf of the Eire Government at 6.20 p.m., and the Union Jack was lowered. The British soldiers then went aboard the motor vessel Innisfallen *and left for Fishguard, a salute being fired as the vessel departed. "The British had already departed when Mr. de Valera and Mr. Frank Aiken, the Minister for Defence, arrived in a launch, being greeted by a salute of 19 guns. The troops were formed up around the flagstaff and Mr. de Valera ran up the tricolour national flag of Eire over Westmoreland Fort to the accompaniment of a salute of 21 guns. As the flag was broken there were cheers, echoed by the thousands gathered on the mainland. Simultaneously the flag was saluted at barracks in Dublin, the Curragh, Athlone and other military centres. The warship* H.M.S. Acasta, *which has been in the port on duty, left about the time the* Innisfallen *sailed, and both were well out to sea by the time the Irish flag was hoisted on the island."*

THE EMERGENCY

Officially, the Irish State was neutral during World War II, but declared a state of emergency on 2nd September 1939 and enacted the Emergency Powers Act the following day.

With Coast Lines being a British company, its ships were committed to the war effort and, although Irish registered, shortly after the outbreak the B&I ships were removed from their normal routes. In fact, until then ships registered at Irish ports flew the Red Ensign; it was only after the declaration of war that the Irish Government established an Irish Register and Flag. The war was also the reason behind the formation of the deep-sea company Irish Shipping Ltd. to bring in the country's imports. In February 1941 the Minister for Supplies, Seán Lemass, stated that "the creation of an Irish mercantile marine was necessary as it was as important as the Army for national safety."

With ships redeployed, and limited tonnage available, B&I had to work hard to maintain services. Passenger services between Cork and Fishguard were suspended, the *Innisfallen* making the last crossing from Fishguard on 26th September 1939 and thereafter used mainly at Dublin while the *Kenmare*, the *Lady Connaught* and the *Lairdscastle* were employed alongside the *Munster*. During this time the *Kenmare* continued a cargo and cattle service from Cork to Fishguard and Liverpool.

The first war casualty to rock B&I was the *Munster*. Transferred to the Belfast-Liverpool service to replace the requisitioned *Ulster Monarch,* she struck a mine early on the morning of 7th February 1940 some 20 miles from the Bar Lightship at the entrance to the River Mersey. Thankfully, all 250 passengers and crew survived.

The next loss was the *Meath* (ex *Lady Meath*). Just before midnight on 15th August 1940 she sailed from Dublin for Birkenhead with 781 cattle and 1,008 sheep aboard. Her first call was Holyhead to obtain clearance from the Naval Control Service. This done, an explosion rocked the ship as it detonated a mine close to the end of Holyhead breakwater, and she went down a mile north-east of the lighthouse. Three men, including Captain Thomas MacFarlane, were wounded but all hands cleared the ship in the port lifeboat and 20 minutes later, having been picked up by the HMS *Manx Lad*, they witnessed the *Meath* sink with the animals still aboard.

The wreck of the *Meath* in Holyhead Bay is now marked by a buoy known locally as 'Meath' and is quite close to the 'Clippera' mark and lies at 53°20.5'N 4°36.4' W. The bow is intact and stands 8 metres proud of the seabed and retains an anchor and chain. The bridge lies on the seabed to port of the wreck and the ship's twin

The first B&I purpose-built ship for the Liverpool run, the *Lady Louth* came from the Ardrossan Dockyard Company in 1923. (John Hendy Collection)

boilers are recognisable. Two gantries stand 5 metres above the seabed at the collapsed stern. At the time of its loss, the ship's position was given as bearing 039.5 degrees, 7.5 cables from the Holyhead outer breakwater light.

On the Cork services, the *Ardmore* sailed for Fishguard on 11th November 1940 with a full load of cattle. When she failed to arrive at the Welsh port, a search was launched but to no avail, and two weeks later one of her empty lifeboats was discovered on a Welsh beach. The wreck of the *Ardmore* was finally located in 1998, not far from the Saltee Islands and the Conningbeg Light. The damage she'd sustained was consistent with an exploded mine.

On 21st December 1940 tragedy struck again. While outbound from Liverpool the *Innisfallen* struck a mine off the Wirral shore near New Brighton and went down with the loss of four crew. Fortunately, no passengers were killed and all 157 and the remaining crew were rescued. But for the remainder of the war the passenger service was cancelled and not reinstated until 22nd May 1946.

As for the *Leinster*, she was re-registered in Liverpool during September 1940 and utilised for hospital ship duties. Initially based in Iceland, she was moved to the Mediterranean as a troop ship and served at Anzio, assisting in the recovery of survivors from the *St David*, a vessel of the Fishguard & Rosslare Railways and Harbour Co. The *Leinster* survived the war and, renamed *Ulster Prince*, returned to peacetime duties – not with B&I but with the Belfast Steamship Co., remaining in service between Belfast and Liverpool until she was sold in 1967.

NEW SHIPS

After the war B&I began to rebuild its fleet, the *Longford* (ex-*Lady Connaught*) and the *Louth* (ex-*Lady Munster*) entering service on the Dublin-Liverpool route from 22nd May 1946 pending the construction of new ships.

The first to arrive from Harland & Wolff was the *Munster* (IV), delivered on 17th January 1948. Before taking up her position on the Liverpool run she was used on the Cork-Fishguard service, revealing the new livery which the *Innisfallen* would wear. Sporting a dark green hull over orange boot topping, cream upper works and green, white and black funnel, the *Munster* certainly brought a splash of colour to the River Lee.

B&I introduced the third *Innisfallen* in June 1948. She was built by Wm Denny & Co at Dumbarton and registered at Cork. As with her predecessor, her service from Cork was on Monday, Wednesday and Friday, returning from Fishguard on Tuesday, Thursday and Saturday respectively. The ship lay over during the day at Cork's Penrose Quay and at Fishguard, putting to sea at night.

The *Lady Leinster* on the Dublin and Liverpool nightly express service. Built in 1912 as the *Patriotic* for the Belfast Steamship Co, she was transferred to B&I in 1930. (John Hendy Collection)

Cork's *Innisfallen* of 1930, lost in the River Mersey in 1940. (John Hendy Collection)

In 1952 Coast Lines welcomed the splendid *Irish Coast*, primarily for the services of Burns & Laird but carrying the colours of Coast Lines – black hull, white upperworks and a black funnel with white chevron. She was the Irish Sea relief ship, providing overhaul cover every year during December, January and February. In 1953 the *Innisfallen* returned from overhaul at her builder's yard displaying the full colours of the City of Cork Steam Packet Company and was warmly received for her white black-topped funnel, white upperworks, black hull with white trim and red boot topping. So too was the return of the City of Cork SPCo house flag, despite the ship and operation remaining in the ownership of B&I.

The *Kenmare* was also returned to City of Cork colours during her dry docking and, having consistently served her owners with excellent reliability, she was retired on 17th May 1956. After completing discharge the old girl sailed across Cork Harbour to Passage West where, on arrival, Haulbowline Industries commenced her demolition.

Replacing the *Kenmare* was the *Glengarrif*, built in 1936 as the *Rathlin* for Clyde Shipping. After service with Burns & Laird as the *Lairdscraig* she made Cork her new home and, having been nursed along there for 7 years, she too ended her days at Haulbowline Industries – as the final passenger ship on the Cork-Liverpool route. The

last days of the Cork-Liverpool service were played out by another elderly vessel – the freight ship *Glanmire*, which commenced the countdown on 11th December 1963.

FLAGGING UP CONTROL FOR IRELAND

In February 1960, a motion in Dáil Éireann – one of the Houses of the Irish Parliament – made a strong case for the proposal that a substantial proportion of the cross-Channel shipping trade should be brought under Irish control to benefit the economy accordingly.

At this time the flag of Irish Shipping Ltd (ISL) flew in every ocean of the world and it was the proclaimed intention of the Irish Government and ISL to further expand the fleet. However, the Irish flag was notably absent from the busiest routes – those linking Ireland

The *Innisfallen* of 1948 and the *Irish Coast*. (Brian Cleare Collection)

The *Munster* of 1938. Just two years later the ship became a casualty of the World War II. (John Hendy Collection)

and Britain.

The government eventually decided that the intervention of an Irish State shipping service on the Dun Laoghaire-Holyhead route would be ineffectual because any Irish service would control only the three or so hours at sea on the 10-hour journey between Dublin and London. Interestingly, Mr Erskine Childers, Minister for Transport and Power, made the announcement at the annual dinner of the Dun Laoghaire Chamber of Commerce, situated on British Railways' doorstep and overlooking the Holyhead mail service terminal. While taking British Railways to task over standards of travel on its mail boats (on a route travelled by almost a million passengers a year), he scotched the one solution which many felt was long overdue – the establishment of an Irish state or semi-state organisation to deliver the kind of service that such an important tourist route demanded.

In 1965 the British & Irish Steam Packet Company Ltd, together with its subsidiary, the City of Cork Steam

D'Innis!

Cork folk have a tendency to shorten every name – and if it happens to have only one syllable they'll shorten it to the first letter! The *Innisfallen* (known affectionately as *D'innis*) was a sort of lifeline connecting so many people from the Munster region on the emigration route to England. Her berth on Penrose Quay was so close to the city that farewells, of which there were plenty, encouraged entire families to wave off their loved ones, particularly given the convenience of early evening sailing times. The ship swinging her stern around into the south channel, before proceeding past Ford, Dunlop and Marina, prolonged the handkerchief waving, and

for me it was also a good time to enjoy the trip down river and say farewell to my

"Dear old Cobh...leaning her back up against the hill, with the tips of her toes in the ocean."

On the smaller *Kenmare* the cattle and cargo were more prominent than on *D'innis*, and the lack of stabilisers was also noticeable! When I went aboard the *Kenmare* and saw the fold-up guards around the dining tables, I knew we were in for a rough crossing. But her time-keeping was impressive and there was a great air of friendliness aboard.

David Walsh

The splendid *Irish Coast* of 1952 proudly displays the colours of Coast Lines. She was the Irish Sea relief ship, providing overhaul cover during the winter months. (John Hendy Collection)

Packet Company, was sold by Coast Lines to the Irish Government. Coast Lines was itself acquired by the P&O Group in February 1971 – a takeover which brought Coast Lines together with its long-time rival the General Steam Navigation Company, part of the P&O Group since 1920. Both companies were restructured to form P&O Short Sea Shipping, which later became P&O Ferries.

By 1951 Coast Lines had a fleet of 109 ships carrying four million tons of cargo, more than half a million head of livestock and over a million passengers, marking the high point in the British cross-Channel freight and passenger trades. But although the company pioneered unit load traffic in the post-war period, Coast Lines failed to embrace vehicle ferries and went into a steady decline. By the mid-1970s most of the former Coast Lines identities and liveries had ceased to exist.

Another view of the *Munster*, showing her buff-coloured hull. (John Hendy Collection)

Chapter six

B+I
Line

In 1965, at a time of great technological change and competition in shipping, the British & Irish Steam Packet Company was bought from Coast Lines Ltd. by the Irish Government for IR£3.6m. The main objective was to maintain and improve services and to ensure competition in sea transport between Ireland and the UK. Indeed, for many in the Irish Government it was in the strategic interests of the country to own and control its own short-sea shipping fleet and to operate it on strictly commercial lines, providing and developing a modern, efficient, profitable and national system of sea services to and from the country.

The B&I fleet at the time comprised the following vessels: the *Leinster* (IV), passenger and cargo ship, 1948; the *Munster* (IV), passenger and cargo, 1948; the *Innisfallen* (III), passenger and cargo, 1948; the *Meath* (IV), cargo, 1960; *Kilkenny* (III) cargo, 1937; the *Glanmire*, cargo, 1936; *Dundalk*, cargo, 1939; the *Wicklow* (II), cargo, 1938 and the *Inniscara* (II), cargo, 1948.

Thus the fleet which the Government acquired was largely obsolete, the ships each having an average age of almost 18 years, and it was soon apparent to the Board that the company would have to be equipped with a completely new fleet, along with specialised modern port facilities.

The post-takeover new investment programme duly set out a variety of key objectives: to transform the company's outdated image, to replace old ships, to introduce drive-on/drive-off car ferries and to mechanise cargo handling systems. The Government duly released a stream of funds into the restyled B+I Line, blissfully unaware that in time the stream would become a cascade.

Outwardly, it fell to the *Innisfallen* to first display any change of ownership by returning from her 1966 annual overhaul with new funnel colours. Gone was the very smart white and black funnel and in its place was a royal blue scheme with a white logo consisting of a right-pointing arrow inside a broken circle. The new look could hardly be considered attractive and by 1967 the black-topped white funnel of the City of Cork SPCo replaced it, also incorporating a new arrow emblem painted in orange – a new livery which was applied across the fleet. Arrows seemed to be in vogue at that time, British Rail having introduced its new double-arrow emblem two years earlier, although – unlike BR, which reversed its arrow on the port side of funnels to point forward –B+I did not, the port side of its funnels having the arrow pointing astern.

On 16th May 1967, the B+I Line Chairman, Liam St John Devlin, issued a statement confirming the withdrawal from the Liverpool service of the *Munster* (IV) and the *Leinster* (IV), and of the *Innisfallen* (III) from the Cork-Fishguard service. First for withdrawal were the *Munster* and the *Innisfallen*, both decommissioned in October of that year. The *Leinster* continued in service into 1968, running three sailings a week in each direction. She left Dublin for the last time on 15th November, bound for lay-up at Birkenhead. The ship had served the Liverpool run well for her 20 years

the ships), the decision to switch the Welsh terminal from Fishguard to Swansea was imposed on the company by the owners of the port, British Rail. The reason given by BR for withdrawing operating rights into Fishguard was that it regarded the new B+I ferry service from Cork as an "unfriendly act".

Alongside in Dublin, the Leinster displays B&I Line's new livery of 1967. (Ian Collard)

and in that time logged some 1.5 million nautical miles and carried over 4 million passengers. It is said that over the years she had transported the rich and the famous and, on one notable occasion, President De Valera found himself sitting opposite the official British hangman!

After a short time in lay-up the *Munster* was sold on 24th July 1968 to Epirotiki of Greece for service in a somewhat warmer climate. The *Innisfallen* was purchased by Greek operator Hellenic Med Lines and renamed *Posedonia*. She was followed to the Mediterranean by the *Leinster*, which was handed over to HML on Christmas Eve 1968.

While Fishguard did not have a linkspan to accommodate the new car ferry service (and neither did Cork or Dublin until they were specifically provided for

The first Board of B&I Line 1965. Seated left to right: Kevin Briscoe, Dr T Beere (Secretary of the Department of Transport & Power), Erskine Childers (Minister of Transport & Power), Liam St.John Devlin (Chairman) and P H Greer. Standing left to right: T A Moran, Diarmuid O'Riordain, P. J O'Brien and Dr Juin Greene.

The first of the new car ferries; the *Munster* on passage to Ireland from her builders in May 1968. (FotoFlite)

Consequently, B+I entered into an agreement with the Swansea Port Authority for the car ferry to operate to and from Swansea, ending direct rail- connected services.

The withdrawal of the old *Innisfallen* caused a backlash in Cork which, pending delivery of new tonnage, was left with no regular passenger service to

Britain. Such was the local anger at temporarily losing the service that a committee of local people looked to British Rail to charter its North Sea vessel *Avalon* for a passenger service to and from Fishguard between 23rd and 29th December. But at the eleventh hour, due to lack of support, the proposal was cancelled.

Cork was also the centre of controversy when B+I

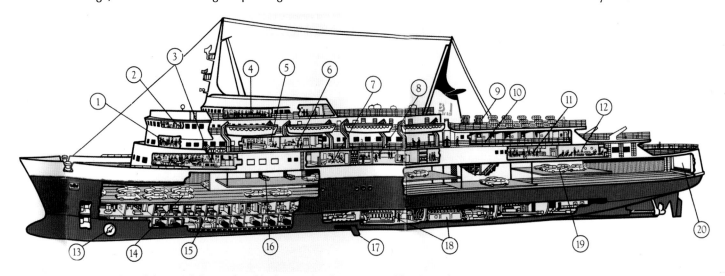

A cutaway view of the *Innisfallen* produced in the B + I brochure. (Ferry Publications Library)

decided to withdraw the *Glanmire* and cease the Cork-Liverpool service. In the first of many instances of government interference, the closure was put off until April 1969 at the request of Erskine Childers, Minister for Transport and Power.

IRISH SEA MOTORWAYS

The new B+I Board commissioned studies of car ferry services then blossoming across Europe and British Rail's Dun Laoghaire-Holyhead operation was of particular interest. At that time British Rail's *Holyhead Ferry I* offered a hugely popular seasonal car ferry service in addition to the year-round mail boat service. As a result of the studies, three new car ferries were ordered – two built in Germany and one in Cork – and for style and innovation they were years ahead of any other ferry then in service in Irish waters.

Traditional names were retained for the car ferries and builders Werft Nobiskrug at Rendsburg delivered the

first, the *Munster* (V), on 2nd May 1968. The original order to build her came from Sweden's Lion Ferry but while she was under construction agreement was secured for B+I to take her instead. B+I simultaneously placed another order with the yard for a near sister, the *Innisfallen,* purpose-built for the Cork station and then the newest of four vessels to bear that famous name.

The *Munster* entered service between Dublin's new Ferryport and Liverpool in time for the summer peak, and how impressive she looked in the new B+I livery – Celtic blue hull set off by green boot topping, white upperworks and the white black-topped funnel (with arrow logo) which was so familiar in Cork. Marketed as the B+I Line Motorway Service, the *Munster* presented a stark contrast to British Rail's 3-year-old *Holyhead Ferry I.* With her powerful diesel engines (controlled directly from the bridge), stylish Scandinavian lines and drive-

The *Innisfallen* on passage from Swansea to Cork. (FotoFlite)

The *Leinster* outward in the River Liffey for Liverpool. (Don Smith/Pictureships)

through loading via bow and stern doors, the *Munster* was certainly a cut above the stern-loading, steam-powered British Rail ship, the engines of which were controlled by the engine room via electric telegraphs from the bridge.

Speaking at the launch of the *Munster*'s new near-sister the *Innisfallen,* B+I Line Chairman Liam St John Devlin revealed that by 1970 B+I aimed to carry 170,000 passengers, 37,500 cars and 60,000 pieces of freight on the new Cork- Swansea service, and that by 1974 a second ship would join the *Innisfallen* on the link. The *Innisfallen* was the third ship launched for B+I within a 6-week period, the others being her Cork-built sister *Leinster* and the *Kildare*, a chartered container ship built at Lubeck in West Germany.

The *Innisfallen* entered service on 2nd May 1969, sailing to the newly-completed terminal at Swansea. As the ship broke away from Cork's Tivoli terminal at 21.00 sharp, other nearby ships sounded their whistles in salute to the newcomer. Along the banks

of the Lee, cars stopped and people lined the roads at Blackrock as the ship, under the command of Captain Tom Davies, sailed past on her maiden voyage. This was the new breed of Irish ferry, sweeping away the homely comforts of the old favourites in an age of intensive running and easy-to-clean utilitarian accommodation. At 24.5 knots and described as Western Europe's fastest car ferry, the *Innisfallen* cost IR£2.5 million and could carry up to 1,200 passengers and 240 cars.

The *Leinster* (V) completed the trio of three new ships, entering service alongside the *Munster* on 1st

The *Dundalk* was built in 1975 to provide freight capacity for B + I between Liverpool and Dublin. (Capt John McKenna Collection)

In 1979 B + I built the *Tipperary* in partnership with P&O's *Ibex* in Japan. (Ferry Publications Library)

satisfy the demand for freight services. In 1974 B+I concluded an agreement with P&O for the introduction of a new roll-on roll-off service between Dublin and Fleetwood. This resulted in new tonnage for the route in 1979 with the building of the *Tipperary* and the *Ibex* in Japan. The latter was owned and operated by P&O, whilst the *Tipperary* was chartered and operated by B+I. The company also returned to Verolme Cork Dockyard for a new ro-ro vessel. Delivered in 1975, the *Dundalk* was something of an oddity given the P&O agreement. Considerably smaller than the *Tipperary*, she briefly operated to Liverpool until Fleetwood came on stream. Then a series of charters took her all over Europe. She was subsequently offered to Stena Line as part payment for a charter and, renamed the *Stena Sailer*, caused a stir when she returned to the Irish Sea in March 1987 on charter to Sealink!

June 1969. She was five knots slower than her Cork sister but this was acceptable for the Liverpool service.

The traffic profile of the routes operated by B+I Line changed dramatically during the years 1968-1978 as the number of passengers with cars increased, and the company embarked on long-term investment to meet anticipated growth. Two lift-on/lift-off ships were built – the *Wicklow* in 1971 and the *Kilkenny* in 1973 – and operated a container service between Dublin and Liverpool and similarly between Dublin/Cork and Rotterdam, Antwerp, and Le Havre. Even this did not

On the passenger side of the business, B+I's answer to Holyhead's new British Rail ferry *St Columba* was a newbuild from Verolme Cork Dockyard. The conflict between the size limitations of the locks at Liverpool

The *Innisfallen* sails along Cork's River Lee, a beautiful part of the Swansea sailing. (Don Smith/Pictureships)

Astern goes the *Munster* into the Ferryport at Dublin on her evening arrival from Liverpool. (Don Smith/Pictureships)

The *Innisfallen*, like her sister the *Leinster*, offered clean and modern lines in stark contrast to their rivals, British Rail, on the Irish Sea services. (FotoFlite)

and the need for greater capacity was very successfully resolved in the design of the *Connacht*. Negotiations with The Mersey Docks and Harbour Board also saw a terminal move from Carrier's Dock to a new berth in Waterloo Dock in 1980.

ENTER THE CONNACHT

The *Connacht* was launched on 20th June 1978 and entered service between Cork and Swansea on 7th February 1979. She was a most welcome arrival, particularly as the *Innisfallen* had spent much of the 1978 season out of service due to engine problems. In her absence the handsome *Stena Germanica*, on charter from Stena Line, maintained the Swansea service.

The *Connacht*'s time on the route was only a matter of months. On 21st May 1979, on completion of B+I's agreement with Swansea Port Authority, she switched to the new Welsh terminal at Pembroke Dock. As

passenger, car and cargo traffic developed, B+I had examined other Welsh ports which could reduce port-to-port sailing time and achieve its objective of operation on short cross-Channel routes.

Bill Mulligan, General Manager, B+I line in 1982.

The Jetfoil *Cu na Mara* nearing completion at the Boeing complex in Seattle. (The late Capt Wesley McDonagh Collection)

Main foyer of the *Connacht*. (Bruce Peter/Irish Ferries)

With the *Connacht* in service, the *Innisfallen* joined the *Leinster* and *Munster* on the Dublin-Liverpool service but her stay in Dublin was brief. The 'troubles' in Northern Ireland caused a dramatic fall in tourist numbers and a 3-ship service could not be justified. In 1980 the *Innisfallen* was sold to Corsica Ferries and renamed *Corsica Viva* for service in the Mediterranean. In early 1995 she briefly operated for Meridian Ferries between Folkestone and Boulogne under the name *Spirit of Independence*. On 17th October 2004 – by then

known as *Derin Deniz* – she completed her last voyage, arriving at Alang in India to be scrapped.

In 1980 the *Connacht* transferred to the Dublin-Liverpool service and was replaced at Cork by the smaller *Leinster* which, in keeping with tradition, was renamed *Innisfallen* (V), thereby releasing the name for another new vessel to be constructed at Verolme. Why the *Innisfallen* (IV) was sold in preference to the *Leinster* was down to its greater speed, making it a more attractive proposition on the sale lists.

The *Connacht* is manoeuvred to the fitting out berth after launch in June 1978 at Verolme Cork Dockyard. (Ferry Publications Library)

The *Connacht* outwards through Cork Harbour for Pembroke Dock. (Don Smith/Pictureships)

By acquisition of its new car ferries in 1968-9, state-owned B+I Line had demonstrated that it was a most progressive and ambitious company. This was evident again in 1980 with the bold introduction of a fast-ferry Irish Sea service. Hovercraft had operated on the English Channel in the late 1960s and early 70s, and the B+I Board established a subsidiary company known as Irish Sea Hovercraft Ltd. An evaluation of hovercraft and other fastcraft resulted in the 1978 order to Boeing for a Jetfoil – a craft developed for both military and civil use and featuring a fully-submerged foil. Named *Cu na Mara (Hound of the Sea)*, it was delivered to B+I in Seattle and transported across the Atlantic as deck cargo on the container ship *Antonia Johnston*. In service, the Jetfoil carried up to 257 passengers (no vehicles) on her city-to-city crossing between a new terminal at Dublin's Custom House Quay and the Prince's Landing Stage near Liverpool's Pier Head – a journey of 3 hours 10 minutes. The service commenced in June 1980 with two return crossings a day.

NEW ROUTE FROM ROSSLARE

The summer of 1980 also saw the opening of a new

route from Rosslare to Pembroke Dock. The possibility of operating such a service had been long in the minds of B+I Line management but the limited facilities at Rosslare could not cater for additional traffic. It was the construction of the port's new west pier, with a linkspan on the east side, which paved the way for B+I's move.

The *Connacht* alongside at Cork's Tivoli Ferryport. (Ferry Publications Library)

The chartered Thoresen ferry *Viking III* inward bound from Rosslare arriving at Pembroke Dock in August 1980. (Miles Cowsill)

The route commenced on 23rd May 1980 using Townsend Thoresen's *Viking III*, which was sub-chartered from Kalmar Line, and it operated until the end of September. The ship was replaced by the *Stena Nordica*, but an industrial dispute over manning levels meant that she didn't enter service until 16th October. A month later (18th November) she suffered engine failure and was subsequently towed to Cork for six weeks of repairs. In the interim, the *Innisfallen* covered some sailings while maintaining her normal run from Cork. Irish Continental Line's *Saint Patrick* took over the link on charter from 2nd December and maintained the service until a temporary suspension on 15th January 1981, the *Stena Nordica* eventually resuming sailings on 2nd February.

By and large, B+I Line found itself with a ferry fleet unable to carry out its scheduled services, and the charters (often of ships ill-suited for the task) continued. And on 23rd April 1981, before the *Stena Nordica* completed her charter, she ran aground in Milford Haven but managed to free herself, leaving two weeks later for service in Canada.

Meanwhile the Jetfoil fastcraft *Cu na Mara*, which

had a troubled first year ending prematurely with her withdrawal for the winter months, returned to service in May 1981. She immediately set a record of 2 hours and 50 minutes for the crossing (of 126 nautical miles) to Liverpool. However, any celebration was tempered by the news that the company expected to make losses of IR£2.8 million in that year, prompting chief executive Bill Mulligan to seek, in vain, a winter charter for the *Cu na Mara* in warmer climes. Originally it had been hoped to run her for 11 months of the year but this was reduced to just five. Despite this, Mr Mulligan expressed a hope to acquire a second, more-up-to-date Jetfoil better suited to operating in most weather conditions. The *Cu na Mara*'s second season brought her B+I career to a premature end. Proving too costly to operate, and unsuitable for Irish Sea

The *Connacht* heads out from Cork to Swansea during her first season in 1979.
(Ferry Publications Library)

The chartered Swedish-flag *Stena Nordica* arrives at Pembroke Dock from Rosslare in 1981. (Miles Cowsill)

conditions, she was laid up in Arklow for a number of years, pending sale, and when the Israeli military expressed keen interest (which came to nothing) it caused some uproar within government! From B+I's point of view the *Cu na Mara*'s acquisition had proven an unfortunate and costly exercise, and she subsequently operated in Japanese waters with the new name *Ginga*.

As for the new *Leinster* (V), there was trouble brewing over the matter of her construction at Cork's

The *Leinster* alongside at Cork during her day layover at the port. (Ferry Publications Library)

Verolme yard. B+I's management realised that both she and the *Connacht* before her could have been built outside Ireland at significantly lower cost, and were furious to discover that the new *Leinster* had long been promised to Verolme to keep jobs at the ailing yard. The Government argued that the orders brought the volume of business given by B+I to Verolme since 1967 to almost IR£60 million – a vital boost for the local labour market.

Launched on 7th November 1980, the *Leinster* (V) was almost identical to her sister ship. The sour taste on the B+I Board's palate lasted throughout her construction and on 4th June 1981 Bill Mulligan announced that he had informed Verolme that B+I would refuse to take delivery of the IR£22.5 million ship because the yard could not guarantee the delivery date, scheduled for that month, and as there was considerable doubt about her readiness the company no longer wanted the ship for the 1981 season. While Verolme digested this news, B+I proceeded with a charter of the *Prinsessan Desirée* for the Rosslare-Pembroke Dock service in lieu of the *Munster*, which was maintaining the Liverpool run pending the arrival of the new ship. The company accepted and the *Leinster* entered service under the command of Commodore Gerald Barry on 3rd July. This in turn finally released the

The *Innisfallen*, ex *Leinster*, on her lunchtime arrival at Pembroke Dock from Rosslare. (Miles Cowsill)

Munster to Rosslare and the return of the *Prinsessan Desirée* to her owners – but not before B+I sub-chartered her to Sealink for 4 weeks.

In October 1981 it was announced by the Minister for Transport that the new Chairman of B+I would be Francis Boland, previously (between 1974 and 1977) a director of the company. He replaced Michael O'Keefe, retiring at his own request.

SHORT-SEA QUEST

The climate in which the debt-laden B+I was now trading demanded a radical rethink. There was still a market for passengers who wanted to sleep whilst the ship was on passage, and the 7 hours at sea on the Dublin and Cork routes satisfied this need, but there was a big question mark over the economics of having two ships idle all day – one in Dublin and one in Liverpool – as a consequence.

Hence the company's strategy for 1982 was focused on achieving a combination of key objectives: rationalisation of services, reducing costs, maximising operating assets and realising saleable assets. And in order to use the fleet to best advantage, a move to short-sea services was essential.

It was around this time that P&O was also seeking to close its loss-making Belfast-Liverpool service, prompting former Minister for Transport Albert Reynolds to suggest that B+I should consider taking it over. He went further by proposing a four-point plan to save the Cork-Pembroke Dock service from closure and to retain the Jetfoil even if it made a loss. Although these proposals were all contrary to rationalising the company's operation, Reynolds made the point that B+I was a national asset with the capacity to serve the country in even greater ways in the future. "Even in the most difficult times," he said, "the spirit of enterprise should

Irish Continental Line's *Saint Patrick* at Pembroke on charter to B+I Line in January 1981. (Miles Cowsill)

The chartered *Prinsessan Desiree* alongside at Rosslare, June 1981. (Miles Cowsill*)*

be awake to new opportunities and ready to acknowledge and rectify past mistakes."

P&O's Belfast-Liverpool service closed and the *Ulster Prince* and *Ulster Queen* were sent to Ostend to lay up prior to sale. The route did indeed reopen but, as the following chapter (*By Sea to France*) describes, not with B+I at the helm.

TO HOLYHEAD ONCE MORE

Owned and operated by the nationalised Sealink UK Ltd, the port of Holyhead became available to B+I Line through the British Government's open ports policy. With a mid-afternoon arrival and departure, B+I could operate a return sailing each day, using the Liverpool ship which otherwise would have laid over in Dublin.

With agreement between the two parties the *Connacht* arrived at Holyhead for berthing trials on 2nd March 1982. Local dockers, and others who felt that their jobs were under threat because of the rundown

of the local marine workshops, took to small boats to blockade the port. Two days later the *Connacht*, this time carrying passengers and cars, was again prevented from berthing. A further attempt was made on 8th March, under the command of Captain Frank Devaney, but to no avail. After three unsuccessful attempts to commence the service, B+I Line staff across the company were frustrated, particularly those on the *Tipperary*, inbound from Fleetwood, and on the *Munster*, alongside in Dublin.

Tempers began to boil over and the *Tipperary* was ready to divert to Dun Laoghaire harbour to prevent access to any Sealink ferry attempting to enter, but with a cargo of perishables onboard the action was called off and the ship continued to Dublin. Instead it was left to the *Munster*, laid up in Dublin following an annual survey, to sail across the bay on hearing of events in Holyhead and anchor off the mouth of Dun Laoghaire harbour. The Sealink vessel *St David*, under the command of Captain Idwal Pritchard, arrived at the port at 18.25 and made her first attempt to pass the *Munster*. However, the Irish ship's Master warned on the radio that there were dinghies between his ship, the harbour wall and the *St David*.

When her first effort to squeeze past failed, the *St David* moved astern. At 18.45 she approached again,

Alongside in Liverpool's Trafalgar Dock is the *Leinster*. (Miles Cowsill)

heading for a gap between the blockading vessel and the piers but immediately, the *Munster* moved to prevent her progress. The *St David* continued her approach and stopped very close to the *Munster*, before backing off again and lining up for another run. Two further attempts were made; first a quick dart for the

Munster's stern, then a run at the bow, but each time the anchored *Munster* blocked her. This pantomime between two growling sea dogs continued for more than an hour before the *St David* sat off for awhile and then returned to Holyhead for stores.

On the following morning, with Captain Pritchard

The *Munster* is dwarfed by the Fleetwood ro-ro *Tipperary*. (Gordon Hislip Collection)

remaining on the bridge, the *St David* again tried to berth at Dun Laoghaire but the *Munster* was still in position across the harbour mouth. The stand-off continued until the *St David* was finally allowed to enter, allegedly to land a sick passenger. Sealink sailings were then suspended, and B+I Line deferred introduction of the new service pending resolution of the dispute. Negotiations between the two companies, with trade unions representing the staff involved, were protracted. Agreement was reached, but not before 38 dockers employed by Sealink at Holyhead were dismissed as a consequence of their actions. It was not until 5th April that the *Connacht* successfully completed berthing trials and on the following day the *Leinster* inaugurated commercial sailings between Dublin and Holyhead.

As for the Master and officers of the *Munster*, when the ship returned to Dublin's North Wall the media were awaiting them, intent on interviewing the Master. After securing her to the wall the crew disembarked one by one, telling the press that the Master would be the last one to come down the gangway. "He's still aboard but will be coming ashore shortly," was their parting promise. Hours after everyone had left the ship, the press were still waiting, having been well and truly duped.

THE WAY AHEAD

In May 1982 the Chairman's statement on B+I results for the year ended 31st December 1981 highlighted the main points of the Operating Plan then in place. The Plan, he said, "is designed to reduce permanently B+I cost structures, maximise the use of operating assets and realise saleable assets to alleviate cash difficulties." He outlined the Plan's main features as follows:

- Commencing a daily Dublin-Holyhead short-sea service in conjunction with a Dubin-Liverpool nightly service.
- Operating a split service from Pembroke Dock, serving Cork and Rosslare with one ship.
- Ceasing groupage services in Cork and selling the surplus assets involved.

Standoff at Dun Laoghaire; the *Munster* blocks the way of the *St David*. (Justin Merrigan Collection)

- Suspending the Jetfoil service.
- Selling one car ferry.
- Reducing the number of B+I personnel by approximately 200.
- Negotiating a pay pause.
- Endeavouring to raise base revenue for tourism and freight to more economic levels.
- Implementing a cost reduction programme covering all aspects of B+I's operations.
- Commencing discussions with the Government on capital requirements.
- Obtaining agreement of the Plan with all B+I personnel .

The Chairman said that "Following discussions with personnel and all other interested parties involved, implementation of this Plan is now underway."

Accordingly, in Cork, B+I Line experimented with a service model similar to that introduced successfully on the Dublin-Holyhead and Liverpool routes. The Cork-based vessel, sailing to Pembroke Dock, made a return trip to Rosslare and then sailed back to Cork. On 29th May 1982 a new IR£5 million ferry terminal had opened downstream at Ringaskiddy, built to accommodate B+I but, extraordinarily, at the opening ceremony B+I was conspicuous by its absence, although by this time the company's management had a clear understanding of where the future lay. And the Cork link proved unsuccessful, the service closing on 2nd February 1983 and the *Innisfallen* transferring permanently to Rosslare.

Both Cork and Rosslare routes suffered because problems arose from the unattractive sailing times and disruption to timetables whenever delays occurred due to bad weather or breakdowns. The Rosslare link fared worse than the Cork route; whereas the Cork schedule operated at the same times throughout the week, with departures from Cork at 09.30 and from Pembroke Dock at 22.45, the Rosslare schedule, using the same ship, had to fit in between these Cork sailings. Hence sailing times to and from Rosslare varied – not only in terms of hours (some of which were hardly an inducement to passengers) but even on varying days of the week, three departures leaving Rosslare at 02.00, three arrivals after midnight and one at 03.00.

The Irish Government stepped in yet again, this time to 'persuade' B+I management to run a summer 1983 trial service from Cork. B+I Line's deputy Chief Executive Officer, Tom Ward, blamed Government policy for the company's poor performance and again raised the argument that the *Connacht* and the *Leinster* could have been built far more cheaply at an international yard. The cost of the two ships (IR£40 million) and the Jetfoil (R£6 million) were significant factors in the company's very heavy loss.

Subsequently, the *Fennia* was chartered from Silja Line of Finland and crewed by B+I Line staff (but with an additional Finnish Captain), operating into and out of the new terminal at Ringaskiddy. The service ran six days a week from mid June to mid September, the end of the season bringing closure of the 120-year-old service from Cork. During the season the *Fennia*, complete with indoor swimming pool, created an excellent impression and frequently arrived 45 minutes ahead of schedule. More the pity then that she was not built for the turbulent conditions of St George's Channel and her seakeeping was poor.

1983 also saw the withdrawal of the *Munster*, sold in March to the Petra Navigation Agencies of Jordan and

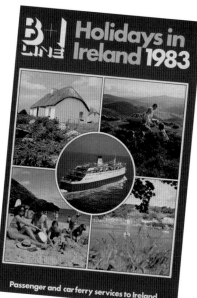

renamed *Farah I.* She operated an 18-hour service from Aqaba to Suez, and also sailings to Jeddah during the Muslim pilgrimage season. In 1990 she was sold to Dalian Steam Shipping Co. Ltd. (China) and renamed *Tian Peng* before her removal from Lloyd's Register of Shipping in 2003.

A VERY MIXED MARRIAGE

The next milestone in B+I's eventful journey could not have been predicted, particularly after the events of March 1982. Sea Containers, new owners of Sealink, which was privatised in 1984, saw that there was unnecessary duplication of sailings on the Irish Sea, and in February 1985 the unimaginable happened: B+I Line and Sealink British Ferries announced a 'pooling' agreement.

The second seasonal Sealink ship at Holyhead was withdrawn and daylight sailings on Sealink's Fishguard-Rosslare route were reduced. B+I's Pembroke Dock operation was suspended during the ship's annual overhaul and the traffic transferred to the British

The *Innisfallen* and *Munster* at Pembroke Dock. (Philip Rodgers)

Displaying the joint service arrangement between B&I and Sealink British Ferries, the British-owned *St Brendan* leaves Fishguard for Rosslare. (Miles Cowsill)

company's *St Brendan.*

All of this was played out against a background of huge public outcry at the liquidation of Irish Shipping by the country's Fine Gael Government. The Minister for Communications, Jim Mitchell, went against the B+I Board's wishes and appointed Zeus Management, a private consultancy firm, with its principal Alex Spain (a former managing partner of the Irish accountancy company Stokes Kennedy Crowley), Chairman and Chief Executive of the company.

On 3rd May 1985 Mr Mitchell announced changes in the chairmanship and management of the B+I Line in Dáil Eireann.

"I am glad to have this opportunity to explain exactly what is involved. I should make it clear at the outset that references to privatisation of the B+I, or to a handing over of control or management of the company, are totally incorrect. There has been no change in the status of the B+I as a State-sponsored body, and it remains a wholly-owned State company. Indeed, the exceptional moves I have made are designed to ensure the future of the B+I.

"Furthermore, the control and direction of the B+I remains with the board of the company, comprising 12

directors, including four worker-directors. Their status, their role and their responsibilities remain unaltered.

"It is completely wrong to suggest that Zeus Management Ltd. will have control of the B+I. The relationship with Zeus Management has two aspects. Firstly, Zeus has been retained by me for a 3-year period to review the business and operations of the B+I Company and, taking account of the need to maintain Irish participation in cross-Channel passenger and freight services, to identify the measures necessary to restore the company to profitable operation by the end of 1986.

"The second aspect is that as part of the overall consultancy arrangement, Mr. Alex Spain, who is the principal in the recently-formed management company, is being appointed Chairman and Managing Director of the B+I Company for the same 3-year period.

"Both these aspects were the subject of very full discussions with the designated sub-committee of the board, including the outgoing chairman. It was acknowledged that the consultancy arrangement was a matter for me as Minister and that the board of the B+I did not have to formally endorse any such consultancy or be a party to the consultancy contract."

After the first summer of pooling the agreement

between B+I Line and Sealink British Ferries was revised. Sealink's *St. Columba* would continue operating to Dun Laoghaire from Holyhead whilst the *Leinster* and *Connacht* would provide two round trips a day between them, alternating with the Liverpool service. Also included was an agreement for covering annual overhaul periods. At Holyhead, the *St. Columba* was due to sail for her annual overhaul in January 1986 and there would be no Sealink ship to replace her. Instead, the *Leinster* would cross the bay to Dun Laoghaire and operate from there to Holyhead while the *St. Columba* was away. B+I's crews were immediately up in arms and insisted that if they were going to do the work of the Sealink ship, they should be paid the same rate as that of the Sealink crews. On the very day the *Leinster* was due to berth in Dun Laoghaire, Sealink was forced to cancel the *St. Columba*'s overhaul and instead she was sent north to Govan for a 24-hour dry docking to renew her passenger certificates.

In the St George's Channel, the Rosslare-Pembroke Dock service ceased with the 02.15 sailing from Pembroke Dock on 5th January 1986, resulting in the loss of 525 jobs. A 'superferry' was to be acquired and operated jointly with Sealink to Fishguard, but as this proposal failed to materialise the *Innisfallen* would partner the *St Brendan,* B+I sailing into Fishguard for the first time since 1968. But before that could happen the overhaul agreement was hit by strike action, forcing Sealink to bring Folkestone's *Vortigern* around to release the *St. Brendan* for attention. When she returned she was sporting a joint Sealink/B+I Line livery.

Another feature of the agreement between the two companies was extensive refits of the main vessels. The *Connacht* and *Leinster* were refitted to the specification of S.H. Sorensens Arkitektkontor AB of Sweden, each emerging with reduced cabin capacity, a new interior layout in passenger areas, and a striking new livery. The former dark blue hulls became mid-blue, topped off by two deep lines of lighter blue at main deck level and rising towards the stern to upper deck level. Superstructures were white and the same colour scheme applied to funnels. The routes served by each ship were detailed in white on its blue hull: Dublin-Liverpool and Dublin-Holyhead on the port side, and Liverpool-Dublin and Holyhead-Dublin on the starboard side. This information appeared on either side of the new B+I Line company logo, in which the + was replaced by an ampersand to become B&I Line. While the *Connacht* and the *Leinster* each received its refit, the *Innisfallen* moved north to deputise in their absence

The *Innisfallen* at Rosslare's new west pier berth. (Miles Cowsill)

and in her place at Rosslare came the chartered Belgian RTM Sealink ferry *Prins Philippe.*

In February 1986 the Government approved equity injections totalling IR£38 million – IR£20 million to be paid in 1986 and IR£6 million in each of the years 1987 to 1989 inclusive, the 1988 and 1989 injections being subject to the achievement by B&I of profit targets determined by the Minister for Communications with the agreement of the Minister for Finance. These profit targets were IR£500,000 in 1987, IR£1 million in 1988 and IR£2 million in 1989. In July (1986), the company changed its name and re-registered as a public limited company – B&I Line plc. A trading loss of about IR£5 million was expected for the year.

Later in 1986 the *Innisfallen* was sold to Greece's Strintzis Lines as the *Ionian Sun.* Strintzis kept her in service until 1998, selling her to Marco Shipping Agency of Dubai, which renamed her *Merdif.* She finally came to the end of the line in 2004, when she was broken up.

Amidst strikes and cancelled sailings, things were already at stretching point when in March 1987 Sealink decided to introduce a freight ship at Holyhead to release space on the *St. Columba*'s car deck. The chartered *Stena Sailer* was no stranger to the Irish Sea – formerly the *Dundalk* of 1975.

For the restyled and bullish B&I Line this was the final straw. As far as the company was concerned, the *Stena Sailer*'s arrival on the scene was a

Dublin sisters, the *Leinster* and *Connacht*. (Gordon Hislip Collection)

breach of the agreement and the Irish Government was called upon to intervene. Subsequently, the state-owned Dun Laoghaire harbour was instructed not to provide facilities for the newcomer. Never before had Irish Sea services been in such a mess. The Sealink freight service was suspended whilst negotiations ensued and was resumed the following month.

Following the sale of the *Innisfallen* to Strintzis Lines, the Fishguard service was again operated by the *St Brendan* while B&I chartered the French (Sealink) vessel *Senlac* to operate one additional daily return sailing during the summer season. By now B&I Line was finding it impossible to reach an acceptable operating and flag-sharing agreement with Sealink and so decided to return to the Rosslare-Pembroke Dock service on the expiry of the agreement in December 1987.

PLANNING FOR SURVIVAL

By this time B&I Line was in serious financial difficulties. The 1986 trading loss had been IR£6.8 million – IR£1.8 million greater than forecast – and far from expecting to meet its modest 1987 profit target,

the company was predicting trading losses of nearly IR£15 million for the year. In May 1987 the Fianna Fáil party Minister for Communications, John Wilson, brought B&I's situation to the Government's notice and on 27th May directed the B&I board to submit an agreed plan of action, for implementation in the autumn, aimed at restoring the company's viability.

B&I had already exhausted the IR£6 million Exchequer equity allocation for 1987 and, to provide time for preparation of the plan of action and to prevent disruption of services during the peak tourism season, the Government agreed additional equity of up to IR£8 million, 75% of which would represent an advance of the 1988 instalment due under the 1986 restructuring package. In the event, the company used IR£5 million of this additional allocation in 1987, recording a loss that year of IR£10.6 million, including financial charges. So in the years 1986 and 1987 the company received IR£31 million in equity. An Exchequer guarantee was also issued during 1987 in respect of bank borrowings of IR£6 million which had been incurred by B&I, with the Minister's consent, in 1986.

The long and very difficult negotiations between B&I management and unions culminated in the submission to the Minister in December 1987 of a Plan of Action. Its main proposals were a reduction of 585 in staff numbers (from 1,464 to 879), a guarantee of industrial peace from the B&I unions until the end of 1990, an across-the-board pay cut of 5% from 1st January 1988, a pay freeze until June 1989, extensive changes in working conditions, and reorganisation of car ferry services.

Under the Plan the Liverpool passenger and car ferry service would close in New Year 1988, an independent B&I Rosslare-Pembroke Dock service resuming at the same time. The Dublin-Holyhead service would intensify, operating two round trips per day on a year-round rather than a peak-season basis.

On the freight side, the company would terminate its involvement in the door-to-door trailer service which it had operated jointly with Pandoro on the Dublin-Fleetwood route. The cumulative effect, taking into account the cost penalty associated with the early termination of the lease on the *Tipperary*, the sale of equipment to P&O, and the settlement with Associated British Ports at Fleetwood, would provide a net yield of approximately IR£1.5 million.

The implementation costs of the Plan mainly comprised redundancy payments, largely financed by the sale of assets, principally the *Connacht*. The bulk of the IR£11 million financing requirement for 1988 related to payments of capital and interest on B&I's existing bank loans and bank overdraft facilities.

On 11th December 1987, having digested the company's proposed Plan of Action, the Government agreed to provide B&I with up to IR£11 million in exchequer equity in 1988 and said that it would review

the position not later than autumn 1988 on the basis of detailed comparisons of the company's performance against forecasts. Naturally, the B&I Board welcomed approval of the plan and the Government's decision to provide continued support. According to Alex Spain, Chairman and Managing Director of B&I, both the workforce and the company were now well positioned to concentrate on the job of marketing its planned new freight and passenger services.

11th December 1987 was also the date on which B&I was set to introduce a freight ship between Rosslare and Fishguard, prompting Sealink British Ferries to cancel its plans to bring freight capacity in the form of the *Earl Harold* around to the link. However, the Greek ship, slated by B&I, was the former Townsend Thoresen vessel *European Gateway* which, some years earlier, had suffered an abrupt end to her UK career when she capsized off Felixstowe following a collision with the Sealink vessel *Speedlink Vanguard*, resulting in the loss of six lives. The wreck was later righted, towed to Greece, rebuilt by her new owners and renamed *Flavia*. With the tragic loss of a further Townsend Thoresen ship, the *Herald of Free Enterprise*, still fresh in everyone's minds, the *Flavia*'s unhappy history was soon brought to B&I's attention, and quicker than you can kick sand from your shoes came the announcement that she had "damaged her bow visor and would not now be coming" to the Irish Sea. This left B&I with a headache in the dying days of the Sealink British Ferries agreement, but the matter was quickly resolved. Belfast Ferries' *Saint Colum I* was lying idle following the collapse of a sale and a charter was quickly arranged, bringing the former Irish Continental Line ship back to Rosslare. The ship ended B&I Line's second association with Fishguard on 12th January 1988. For this short time the former *Saint Patrick* had regained a green funnel, and the following month she was back at Belfast with her red colours restored.

B&I Line duly closed its passenger service to Liverpool on 6th January 1988, so ending the 151-year-old passenger link between Dublin and the Mersey port. The original plan was to close on 10th January, the *Connacht* taking the westbound sailing and the *Leinster* the eastbound. Severe weather over the New Year period caused service disruption, as did engine trouble suffered by the *Connacht* on 5th January, delaying her 22.00 Dublin departure by 4 hours. The crossing was made on just two of her four engines and she was not alongside in Liverpool until the following afternoon. The *Leinster* remained on schedule, arriving in Dublin on the

Left to right: Jim Kennedy (Deputy Chief Executive, Finance); Alex Spain, (Executive Chairman); and Brendan Bird, (Deputy Chief Executive, Operations at B & I) pictured in 1986.

The chartered Belgian RTM Sealink ferry *Prins Philippe* was used on joint Fishguard-Rosslare route in 1986. (FotoFlite)

morning of 6th January. She was immediately turned around to begin twice-daily sailings to Holyhead, and the *Connacht* was repaired before moving south to Rosslare.

The company entered a new agreement with Pandoro for the operation of a joint freight service using two ships on the Liverpool route. Pandoro provided both ships, the *Buffalo* and the *Bison*, the latter on a charter arrangement to B&I, which took over responsibility for operating and crewing her. The European container service was made more cost efficient through the reduction of staff and other savings. The company continued to operate the *Wicklow* and the *Kilkenny*, on services linking Dublin/Cork/Le Havre/Antwerp and Rotterdam.

The days of the *Connacht*, which was taking up service on the reopened Rosslare-Pembroke Dock route, were already numbered. Services on both Holyhead and Pembroke routes now operated with two return sailings a day, though reduced to one return sailing on the 'southern corridor' on certain days outside the peak season. Economies dictated the disposal of the *Connacht*, and at the end of 1988 she was sold to Brittany Ferries, leaving B&I with just one passenger/car

ferry. Renamed *Duchesse Anne*, the former *Connacht* entered service on Brittany Ferries' Portsmouth-Saint Malo route but returned to Irish waters in 1993, 1994 and 1995 on the French company's St Malo-Cork route. The ship subsequently became the *Dubrovnik* when sold by Brittany Ferries for service in the Adriatic.

The *Connacht*'s exit from B&I obliged the company to charter more tonnage – always an expensive exercise

Tthe Belgian RTM vessel *Prins Philippe* arriving at Rosslare in 1986. (Brian Cleare)

– in order to maintain services during the annual overhaul period in February 1989. Into the fleet came Sally Line's *The Viking* but was an unmitigated disaster, breaking down even before she took up Dublin-Holyhead sailings and delaying the *Leinster*'s dry docking by a week. When she *did* enter service, 2 round trips were lost due to bow visor trouble and a week after that *The Viking* failed whilst alongside Holyhead's station berth, forcing a hasty move to the port's container terminal to allow the incoming *St Columba* to berth.

There now followed quite a line of chartered tonnage operating the Pembroke run. Irish Continental Line's *Saint Patrick II* covered off-peak sailings, and the 1971-built *Earl Harold* (ex-*Ailsa Princess*), repainted in B&I Line livery, was chartered from Sealink-Brittany Ferries for the 1989 season. During the high season, the Cypriot-registered ro-ro vessel *Oleander* acted in a support role to the *Earl Harold*, which served until 12th October 1989 and was then returned to her owners. Next, on a short-term charter, pending the arrival of a longer-term replacement, came Faroese company Smyril Line's *Norröna*. While attempting to berth during a particularly nasty winter gale the *Norröna* collided with the linkspan at Rosslare and was diverted to Dublin to discharge her weary passengers and undergo repair. B&I

On charter to Swansea-Cork Ferries, the Greek *Ionian Sun* was none other than the former B+I *Innisfallen*, ex-*Leinster*. (Miles Cowsill)

hastily chartered the Isle of Man Steam Packet Company's diminutive side-loading car ferry *Lady of Mann* to prop up Dublin-Holyhead services with two extra daily round trips from 21st -23rd December inclusive.

Meanwhile, B&I had other battles to fight. It was generally recognised that the company was treated

B&I Line's contribution to the joint service operation at Fishguard was the chartered SNCF ferry *Senlac*. (Miles Cowsill)

The *Leinster* sails through Milford Haven outward bound for Rosslare.(Miles Cowsill)

unjustly with regard to berthing at Holyhead, particularly in comparison with the virtually unrestricted facilities provided at Dún Laoghaire harbour for Sealink British Ferries by the controlling authority there, the Office of Public Works. B&I argued that Sealink's control of both Holyhead and Fishguard dominated the routes and guaranteed its ships on those services the key sailing times. Although at that time there were two terminals at Holyhead, B&I frequently had to use the inadequate terminal at Salt Island. To top it all, B&I's quoted costs of operating in and out of Holyhead were very much in excess of the corresponding charges levied to Sealink at Dún Laoghaire.

The Government strongly supported B&I's case for more equitable berthing facilities and more reasonable port costs at Holyhead. Members considered it unrealistic for the Exchequer to continue to finance B&I in circumstances in which the company was facing unfair competition – and particularly from a rival which was additionally receiving very favourable terms and facilities at Dun Laoghaire, also financed by the Exchequer.

Whenever the prime station berth at Holyhead was

free of Sealink ships, B&I Line took the opportunity to use it. The late Captain Len Evans, Sealink's Senior Master of the *St Columba* (129.2 metres long) and of the port until his retirement in 1986, once told the author of this chapter: "Leaving Holyhead stern first in a southerly gale could be quite hairy, and we had a grudging admiration for the B+I ships (122 metres long)

A publicity picture from B & I shows the *Leinster* at speed outward bound outward from Dublin to Liverpool. (Ferry Publications Library)

Summer 1989 saw Sealink's *Earl Harold* on charter to B&I Line for the Rosslare – Pembroke service. (Miles Cowsill)

which used to do a free swing in the harbour before proceeding out."

Rivalry apart, the spirit of the sea is strong stuff and the co-operation between seafarers on the wave a thing of legend. On 31st January 1990 *St Columba*, on the 08.45 Sealink Dun Laoghaire-Holyhead sailing, suffered a serious engine room fire when 10 miles off the South Stack Lighthouse and senior master Captain John Bakewell issued a Mayday distress call. In addition to the RAF's 22 Squadron, the *Leinster* responded too. With Captain Peter Pope on the bridge, the B&I ship stood by until the stricken vessel was safely alongside in Holyhead Harbour just before midnight and, after a fast turnaround, the *Leinster* sailed for Dublin.

During the early months of 1990, the fire aboard the *St Columba* was the first of a number of such incidents involving ferries in north-western Europe. April was particularly trying, three vessels suffering fire damage within the space of just three days. One (on the 9th) was the *Norröna*, on charter with B&I Line. She was about 30 miles off the Pembrokeshire coast, on passage to Rosslare, when around 04.00 a fire was discovered in the cabins area. Some 30 people were injured and one

passenger later died. The ship returned to Pembroke Dock and passengers were detained by police investigating the incident, arson proving to be the cause of the fire.

Prior to this tragedy, B&I had been looking for a suitable vessel to acquire on long-term charter for the 'southern corridor' route. This eventually materialised in late 1989 in the form of the *Munster,* built in 1970 in the German yard of Werft Norbiskrug, Rendsberg, for Lion Ferry AB of Sweden. The ship's previous names included the *Prinz Oberon* (under which she was well known on the North Sea), the *Feri Malaysia* (operating passenger and vehicle ferry services from the Eastern Malay Peninsula) and the *Cruise Muhibah* (for cruises to Singapore). On closure of the latter services in 1989 she was surplus to requirements and offered for sale. Zatlen Ltd, an Irish company formed specifically for the purpose, bought the ship for a two-year charter to B&I Line. Renamed *Munster* (VI) and registered in Dublin, she sailed from Singapore in January 1990 with a B&I crew under the command of Captain Peter Clarke, arriving (via Suez) in Dublin on 5th February. Although she was in sound condition overall, a minor fire during her IR£3.5

Waters new! The former *Connacht* as the *Duchesse Anne* after sale to Brittany Ferries. (FotoFlite)

million refit fortuitously smoked out very unwelcome stowaways – rats, snakes and cockroaches! She entered B&I service on the Rosslare-Pembroke Dock route on 27th April 1990 and from the outset was well patronised.

Although proving reliable on the Rosslare route, when switching to the Dublin-Holyhead service

A further sale brought the *Connacht* to Croatia as Jadrolinija's Dubrovnik. (Miles Cowsill)

beginning on 13th February 1991 to substitute for the *Leinster* during the latter's annual overhaul, the *Munster* did not fare so well. Slower than the *Leinster,* she also had problems with the linkspan at Holyhead's Salt Island terminal, where the passenger gangway could not be used and foot passengers had to be taken on and off the vessel on buses, causing lengthy delays. This procedure was to become commonplace in later years, due to lack of facilities at the outer berth and prolonged problems at the new berth which opened in 1995.

The *Munster* again covered the *Leinster's* refit in the following year, arriving at Holyhead on 13th February 1992. Things were no better, the added complication of tidal problems commonplace until the opening of the new outer harbour berth. While the *Munster* was in Dublin, and during her own annual overhaul, the *Norröna* operated the Rosslare service, as she had done in 1991.

END GAME

Between 1965 and 1992 the Irish Government invested a total of IR£142.5m in share capital in B&I

The *Saint Patrick II* is seen here leaving Pembroke Dock whilst covering for the absence of one of the B & I vessels on the route in October 1997. (Miles Cowsill)

The Isle of Man Steam Packet Company's *Lady of Mann* was an unusual charter for B&I Line for Christmas 1989. (Miles Cowsill)

Line. By the end of the 1970s, after a decade of losses, the company returned its first profit, but the figures thereafter told a very different story. Even with continuous injections of public funds, the company performed dismally throughout the 1980s, and despite operating receipts increasing tenfold between 1965 and 1978 (from IR£4.3m to IR£42m), B&I Line yielded an annual loss or insignificant profit.

One of the main reasons for the failure of B&I Line was political pressure. As public companies are controlled by Government, they are inevitably held accountable for all major decisions. Thus B&I's management was influenced and second-guessed by the Government in order to achieve political or social

The chartered *Prins Hamlet* inward bound to Pembroke Dock off Angle Bay. (Miles Cowsill)

The *Leinster* goes alongside at Holyhead's Admiralty Pier in Holyhead. (Miles Cowsill)

The *Connacht* inward to Pembroke Dock off Milford Haven. (Miles Cowsill)

A new *Munster* came to the B&I Line fleet in 1990. A handsome ferry, but her aging accommodation was far from ideal. (Miles Cowsill)

The chartered *Norröna* provides overhaul relief at Pembroke. (Miles Cowsill)

The *Leinster* outward bound from Holyhead. (Justin Merrigan)

goals. For example, when B&I tried to end the loss-making Cork-Pembroke Dock service, the Government prevailed in preventing them, at least temporarily.

The overall decline in the company's position may also be attributed to a number of developments which can be summarised as follows:

- Over-expansion in the late 1970s, resulting in increased financial charges and overstaffing.
- Substantial fuel price increases from 1979

onwards, affecting particularly those operators on long cross-channel routes.

- General economic recession in the period 1979–1984.
- Depressed market conditions up to 1985, and intensive competition and price cutting;
- Service disruption due to industrial disputes (mainly in the UK) in the late 1970s and early 1980s.

Loss of the Kilkenny

Throughout 1991, as privatisation approached, there was much speculation about the future shape of B&I Line – all of which, sadly, was to be overshadowed by tragedy.

Shortly after 21.00 on the night of 21st November the container vessel *Kilkenny* was inbound through Dublin Bay from Rotterdam, under the command of Captain Daniel Cummins. Outward from the port with a full cargo of containers was the Danish-owned and German-registered *Hasselwerder*, chartered by B&I. The ships collided with each other 1.5 miles east of the Poolbeg lighthouse.

On picking up the *Kilkenny*'s Mayday, the car ferry *Leinster*, loading at the B&I ferryport in preparation for her 21.45 sailing for Holyhead, immediately put to sea

under the command of Captain Frank Forde. On arrival at the collision scene he directed and co-ordinated the rescue operation, assisted by the Dun Laoghaire and Howth lifeboats. The *Hasselwerder* sustained damage to her bow and bulbous bow, but it was much worse for the *Kilkenny*, holed beneath the waterline. She sank, coming to rest on a shallow sandbank on her port side, and 3 members of her crew died. Captain Cummins was charged with manslaughter but exonerated.

As she was blocking a shipping lane into Dublin Port, the *Kilkenny* was cut up on site. Her anchor is a memorial to those who lost their lives and stands on the lawn which fronts Irish Ferries' Head Office building on Alexandra Road, Dublin.

John Byrne

The *Munster* at Rosslare pending her evening sailing to Pembroke Dock. (Miles Cowsill)

- The introduction in 1986 of airfares deregulation.
- Substantial provisions for losses associated with extraordinary items.
- High finance charges associated with a high/debt equity structure.

The availability of Government finances exacerbated the problems at B&I. Since the threat of bankruptcy did not really exist, the market was prevented from disciplining the company, resulting in over-investment and overstaffing. The eventual restructure and layoffs helped to reduce the company's losses to €1.5m in 1988, but B&I's problems ran much deeper. Between 1985 and 1989 turnover in real terms had fallen by 45%. Even after restructuring, the company could not control staff costs, which in the years 1988–90 rose by

11% – even though in that same period the number of staff fell by 8% .

By 1990 B&I's loss had increased again to €3.6m and it had a capital deficiency of IR£26.5m and a fleet of only two owned ships. It was effectively insolvent, dependent on Government subventions, and with change critical the privatisation of B&I Line was seen as the best solution to cure the company's ills.

A place of work

To many working-class families and communities in Dublin and Cork, B&I Line was an important part of life. I can think of many families from places in Dublin who had 3 or 4 generations that worked for the company – names such as Fay, Brazil, Hutton, Walsh, Gilligan, Lawlor, my own family and many others from Cork, Wexford, Drogheda and all over the country. I don't think it can be overstated how important that

constant employment in the company, both ashore and afloat, was to those families during the bad times from the 1950s to the 1980s. I enjoyed my time there, especially those early years when I had to do a lot of growing up very quickly!

Aiden McCabe

Chapter seven

By Sea
to France

I n October 1967 Ireland's state-owned deep-sea carrier Irish Shipping Ltd announced a new car ferry service direct from the south-east of the country to the north-west of France. As a joint venture between Irish Shipping, London's General Steam Navigation Company and Paris's Societe Anonyme de Gerance et Armament (SAGA), the new link would operate as Normandy Ferries-Irish Continental Line.

On the morning of 19th May 1968 the newly built French-flag ferry *Leopard* arrived off Rosslare. Once alongside and made fast at the new linkspan, provided for the service by port owner Córas Iompair Éireann (CIÉ), the *Leopard* discharged 450 passengers, 110 cars and five trucks. A similar load was awaiting her return sailing to Le Havre.

A national French strike prevented the following weekend's service and on 2nd June it was the turn of the *Leopard*'s British sister, the *Dragon*, to make the crossing. With the strike persisting she sailed from Rosslare but rather than to north-west France took her passengers and cargo to the Portuguese port of Lisbon. It was mid-June before the intended Rosslare-Le Havre sailings could operate again and the service settled into a routine of departing the French side every Saturday at 12.15, the return leaving Rosslare at 12.00 every weekend until 30th September.

The operation was considered a success, which made the news that came along in mid-season 1971 all the more shocking: Normandy Ferries announced that this would be its last summer on the link, due largely to the need to concentrate on its core Southampton-Le Havre service in the face of increasing competition. The final sailing left Rosslare on 11th October 1971, the tally for the season being 32,000 passengers and just over 9,000 cars.

The Irish Government was lobbied by stakeholders for the continuation of the service, the benefits to tourism being considerable. Despite the County Wexford Chamber of Commerce identifying an available ship – Swedish Lloyd's *Saga*, with a price tag of IR£3 million – the 1972 season was lost, the ship going to Stena Line. Amazingly, there was even a suggestion that British Rail's Fishguard side-loading ferry *Duke of Rothesay* might be chartered to reopen the service. Built in 1956 and converted in 1967 to carry cars, this steam turbine was a very far cry from the modern style of the *Leopard* and the *Dragon* – and thankfully the suggestion came to nothing.

While the service was in limbo, B+I Line was doing nothing more than watching from a distance. Eventually, the Government instructed the company to look at the continental run, a request that returned the belief that the Rosslare link was unviable. Irish Shipping, however, had a different view and with clearance from the Government the search for suitable tonnage resumed.

It did not take Irish Shipping long to find a solution, and that lay in the hands of German shipbuilder Schichau Unterweser AG. Lion Ferry had an option on a new ship and after discussion this option was exercised, the ship owned 50% by Irish Shipping, 25% by Lion Ferry and the remaining 25% by Norwegian shipping company Fearnley and Egar. The new ship was to be named *Saint Patrick* and operated by a new company, Irish Continental Line, comprising the three partners. The ICL shareholding was split 30% Irish Shipping, 25% to each of the Scandinavian companies and 20% to CIÉ (Córas Iompair Éireann). Aubrey McElhatton was appointed Managing Director.

The *Saint Patrick* was launched on 17th January 1973 and on 28th May she made her first appearance at Rosslare for berthing trials. She dominated the scene at Rosslare Pier: large, modern and, as if to accentuate her role as the tourism link between Ireland and France, white! Atop the white hull was the buff funnel of Irish Shipping, a St Patrick's cross for Ireland and the Fleur de Lis of France. To signify her joint ownership, the funnel was dressed with a band of blue for Sweden, white for Norway and green for Ireland. Rosslare, the preserve of

Irish Continental Line's new *Saint Patrick* moves up to the ramp at Rosslare for her inaugural sailing in 1973. (Justin Merrigan Collection)

the Fishguard steamers of British Rail, had never before seen such a ship. At 5,285 tons the *Saint Patrick* boasted accommodation for 1,040 passengers, 555 with berths. The vehicle decks, loaded through bow and stern doors, could take 200 cars or 30 trucks, or a practical combination of both.

The ship that started it all; the Leopard in May 1968. (FotoFlite)

The *Saint Patrick* at Rosslare awaiting another summer sailing to France in 1978. (John Hendy

Under the command of Senior Master Captain Ivan Shiel, the IR£5.5 million *Saint Patrick* sailed from Rosslare on her maiden voyage to Le Havre on 2nd June 1973. Curiously, the ship was registered in Wexford, a port incapable of accommodating a vessel of such size! She operated all year round between Rosslare and Le Havre, sailing three times a week in each direction, and on alternate days during the July-August peak. The route was very well patronised, not only by Irish tourists heading mostly for France, but also by continental passengers holidaying in Ireland. Freight hauliers were also

Irish Continental Line celebrate 10 years of service. Photographed at the special reception left to right: Bill ONeill, Chairman of Irish Shipping and Aubrey McElhatton, Managing Director of Irish Continental Line. (ICL)

SPLASH!

The launch of the *Saint Patrick* in Bremerhaven on 17th January 1973 was an interesting affair – a sideways launch into a river no wider than Dublin's Tolka! When the ship dropped down and hit the water, all of it swooshed up on the river bank opposite and the ship keeled over to what seemed to onlookers a perilous degree, and I feared she'd go. Just then Frank Khan, the *Irish Independent* reporter, attending the event with his shipping correspondent John Maddock, quipped, "For one moment, Don, I thought I had a story!"

Don Hall, Hall Public Relations

Looking for a second ship, Capt Colman Raftery found the ideal match for ICL's needs; Stena Line's *Stena Scandinavica* became the *Saint Killian* in 1978. (Ferry Publications Library)

quick to grasp the opportunities provided by the service at a time when Ireland was joining the European Economic Community. So all in all the undertaking was highly successful.

In 1976 Irish Continental Line formed a subsidiary company, Ferrytours, to promote the concept of self-drive package holidays made easy using the car ferry service. A year later the Scandinavian involvement in ICL ceased, and Irish Shipping became 80% owners of the company, with CIÉ retaining its 20% share. Ownership of the *Saint Patrick* was then transferred from Irish Shipping to Irish Continental Line – a fortuitous (and maybe inspired) decision as, in 1984, after 43 years' service to the Irish State, Irish Shipping was to face liquidation. At around this time a new green funnel livery was introduced, featuring a large white shamrock.

During the winter of 1980/81 the *Saint Killian* was dispatched to Amsterdam for stretching. She returned to service as the *Saint Killian II*. (Miles Cowsill)

The *Saint Patrick* on passage from Le Havre to Rosslare. (FotoFlite)

As well as announcing the new status of Irish Continental Line as a company, this also proved to be a powerful marketing tool, creating a memorable and unmistakably Irish brand and corporate identity.

The success of the Rosslare-Le Havre service was proven in 1978 when the company purchased the *Stena Scandinavica* to operate in tandem with the slightly smaller *Saint Patrick* (but before entering service in Irish waters the new acquisition was chartered back to Stena Line until April 1978, after which she visited Dún Laoghaire to promote the route).

Marine Manager Captain Coleman Raftery had searched the ferry world for a suitable ship and he reported to the Board that the *Stena Scandinavica* was perfect for expanding the Ireland-France routes. Built in 1973 at the yard of Titovo Brodogradiliste in Kraljevica, Yugoslavia, she was renamed *Saint Killian* and enabled the company to operate daily sailings between Ireland and France in summer months. Cherbourg was added to the ports served, the crossing time of 17 hours comparing favourably with the 21 hours of the Le Havre service. The new route was well patronised by those holidaymakers from Ireland attracted by western France and the resorts of Brittany and the Vendee.

In the very year that services were expanded, a slump in the international economy heralded a decline in business. The effects of this were compounded by the fact that Rosslare was not the sophisticated facility that it is today, and vessels had to refuel in France, a 20% hike in prices adding £10,000 a day to operating costs.

Capt Ivan Shiel, Irish Continental Line's senior master. (ICL)

BY BELFAST TO ENGLAND

With the stormy waters of the late 1970s behind it, Irish Continental Line was again in expansionist mood, and on 1st May 1982 opened a new service linking Belfast and Liverpool, operated by a further subsidiary called Belfast Car Ferries.

The route had been established for over a century, and was formerly operated by Coast Lines Ltd. and, following its takeover in 1971, by the P&O Group. The P&O service was discontinued at the end of 1981 – the result of the decline in tourist traffic created by the 'troubles' in Northern Ireland. The vessels used at the time were the very traditional *Ulster Queen* and *Ulster Prince* of 1967.

Belfast Car Ferries was incorporated in Northern Ireland as a private company. Chief Executive was John Hewitt, the former Financial Controller of P&O Ferries (Irish Sea). In Dublin, Aubrey McElhatton took on the role of Managing Director, in addition to his position with Irish Continental Line.

It was intended to rename the *Saint Patrick*, but marine authorities objected to the proposed new name of *Saint Columb* on the grounds that it was too similar to the *St Columba* at nearby Holyhead. Taking this into account, and mindful of the potential funding/subsidy from the UK Government, the company registered the ship in Belfast as the *Saint Colum I*. Her altered livery sported a red funnel, with the large white shamrock, as opposed to the company's then traditional green funnels.

Commanded by Captain James (Jimmy) Fullerton, a veteran of the Belfast-Liverpool route for 12 years, the *Saint Colum I* sailed from Belfast's Donegall Quay for Langton Dock in Bootle on 1st May 1982. The ship returned the following morning, so establishing the pattern of a nightly departure from Belfast and a morning return sailing – a schedule which was to deprive the service of lucrative freight traffic on the Belfast-bound sailing, and so affect its viability when competition subsequently arrived.

In 1984 the *Saint Colum I* made 350 voyages and carried 208,000 passengers, 46,056 cars and 7,108 freight units, as well as accounting for 19,000 trade cars (25% of all imports into Northern Ireland). In the same year a new company, Belfast Freight Ferries, was formed, with a service to and from Heysham, and Belfast Car Ferries was appointed local manager. The service was a success and by 1987 there was talk of the ferry being too small and the need for a larger and faster ship.

Things were also changing in Rosslare. Releasing the

The *Aurella*, purchased by ICL in 1982. (Ferry Publications Library)

Saint Patrick for her Belfast role was a newly-acquired ship, the *Saint Patrick II*. Built as the *Aurella* for Viking Line, she was sent to the Netherlands for an extensive refit and conversion at Amsterdamsche Droogdok Maatschaapij. The *Saint Killian* was also sent to ADM for an extensive refit, costing IR£7.5 million and including a 32.5-metre extension to her hull and superstructure, thereby increasing her capacity to 1,400 berths and 380 car spaces. Following this major enhancement she was renamed *Saint Killian II*. And just as she had in 1978, when purchased, she sailed to Dun Laoghaire for a show-the-flag visit for travel agents, berthing there on 9th March 1982. By the time the *Saint Killian II* arrived in Dublin Bay, the blockade that had made national headlines had ended. The B+I ferry *Munster* had left her anchorage, freeing the entrance to Dun Laoghaire harbour and Sealink's *St David* had departed for Holyhead.

The scene was set for a standard and style of service which endured for several years. Commencing in late June 1983, additional sailings to and from Cork's Ringaskiddy Terminal were made during peak summer season and proved very popular, not only with tourists from the Munster area but also with continental visitors to holiday destinations in the counties of Cork and Kerry. Happy days – but lurking around the corner was a bombshell.

Before this, in February 1983, the *Saint Killian II* was in the news when she encountered severe gales – force 9 gusting to force 11 – as she rounded Land's End on passage from Le Havre to Rosslare. A series of heavy seas over the bow smashed a window on the bridge and water entered the wheelhouse, resulting in an electrical fault which affected the ship's steering. A

The *Saint Patrick II* alongside at Cherbourg. (Miles Cowsill)

Mayday call was issued, but cancelled again when the fault was rectified. The ship then diverted to Falmouth for a temporary repair to the damaged window. In April another incident sent *Saint Killian II* to the assistance of the burning Brittany Ferries car ferry *Armorique*, en route to Cork from Roscoff. *Saint Killian II* stood by as some passengers were transferred to shore from the French ship by helicopter and lifeboat. Sadly, one passenger died.

As for the bombshell: following a series of financially disastrous charter deals for Irish Shipping vessels in Hong Kong, the Fine Gael Irish Government liquidated the company in November 1984. Irish Continental Line and Belfast Car Ferries were both returning a profit but this was of no consequence to the liquidator, who put both companies on the market. Two and a half years of uncertainty followed as the search for a buyer went on. One of many consequences was the withdrawal of Belfast Car Ferries' management of the Belfast Freight Ferries operation, the contract handed over to Wallem Ship Management. Finding a buyer for what was a financially-stable operation proved to be more difficult than expected, and in December 1985 the company was advertised for sale in the Irish national press.

Ironically, Irish Continental Line came within the sights of B+I Line for acquisition. As described in previous pages, in 1979 the Minister for Transport informed B+I that the company should not operate a service to the Continent and this was now being advanced as a reason for B+I's problems in Cork. On 22nd February 1983, the Minister of State at the Department of Transport, Mr Donnellan, said that it had been stated that such a (B+I) service (to the Continent) would have been profitable and that the profits could have been used to sustain the service (from Cork) to Britain. B+I had been given an opportunity to become involved in the operation of a service to the Continent following the withdrawal of Normandy Ferries. Irish Continental Line was then set up for this purpose and it would have been unrealistic to have two State shipping companies operating competing services to the Continent. "The argument that denial to B+I of a passenger service from Cork to France lay at the root of the difficulties of the company's Cork-Wales service was often put forward by people who, in the next breath, claimed that B+I and Irish Continental Line should have been amalgamated!" Mr Donnellan said. (*Dáil Eireann Debate Vol. 340 No. 4*)

There were also protracted taxation problems, resulting from the ownership of the *Saint Killian II* and *Saint Patrick II*, but in November 1986 sole title to the vessels was secured. It should be remembered that

The *Saint Killian II* was stretched in ADM, Amsterdam in 1982. On completion she was able to accommodate 2,000 passengers and 380 cars. (Irish Ferries)

A longer saint! The *Saint Killian II* on passage to Ireland from Le Havre. (FotoFlite)

The *Saint Patrick II* at the Terminal d'Irelande at Le Havre. (Miles Cowsill)

The *Saint Colum 1* heads into Langton Lock at Liverpool at the start of her passage to Belfast. (Ferry Publications Library)

during this time the ships continued to sail and crews sustained a quality service to passengers, despite the burden of uncertainty being carried by all company employees, both ashore and afloat.

On Christmas Eve 1986 a fire disabled the *Saint Killian II* off the coast of Cornwall. She was towed to Falmouth for temporary repairs and in January 1987 moved to Blohm & Voss in Hamburg, Germany, for full repairs, resuming service in February.

Eventually, in 1987, a consortium of institutional investors, led by Eamonn Rothwell and NCB Stockbrokers, made a successful bid for the company. The deal for Irish Continental Line and Belfast Car Ferries was completed for IR£4 million and the assumption of IR£12million in debts.

Heading up the new Irish Continental Group plc was Paddy Murphy, formerly of Aer Lingus and recruited in to head up the company. He replaced Aubrey McElhatton, who stepped down as Managing Director. Irish Continental Line was given the new name Irish Ferries and its ships bore a new funnel logo (a white shamrock within a navy blue, green and light blue angular flag, still on the green background) but retained the white hull and green boot topping. Belfast Car Ferries became Belfast Ferries, the white shamrock on the red funnel replaced by the Irish Continental Group flag.

With energy and optimism revived, the newly-reconstituted company set about its business with gusto, and trade grew steadily. New fare structures were introduced to encourage early bookings, along with off-peak savings for passengers and cars, and competitive new tariffs for freight operators. In line with their status as hotels at sea, the ships were extensively refurbished, and in October 1987 a plan to sell the *Saint Colum I* went as far as replacing her with the *Saint Patrick II*, complete with the red funnel of Belfast Ferries. At the eleventh hour, as the clock ticked down on the beginning of the new season, the sale of the *Saint Colum I* fell through and the ships were switched again, the *Saint Patrick II* regaining her green colours. However, there was a brief charter of the *Saint Colum I* to B&I Line, which under the terms of the about-to-expire Sealink partnership was obliged to provide a ship on the Rosslare-Fishguard service, and following this the *Saint Colum I* underwent a major overhaul, again losing her short-lived return to the green colours for red, and she returned to the Liverpool run in ample time to service the 1987 summer peak.

In shipping circles Irish Ferries was widely regarded as a resourceful company. During winter months, when

The *Saint Patrick II* commences her swing at Rosslare before coming astern onto the berth on arrival from France. (Miles Cowsill)

services to France were capably handled by one ship, lucrative alternative employment was usually found for the *Saint Patrick II*, most notably with North Sea Ferries, Tallink, P&O European Ferries and Sealink British Ferries. A regular charter was to B+I Line and on 6th January 1984 *Saint Patrick II* carried out berthing trials at Holyhead prior to taking up the Dublin-Holyhead/Liverpool service while the *Leinster* and the *Connacht* were overhauled. Reputedly holding the record for more changes to her funnel colours than any other north-western European ferry, in 1989 she added B&I Line's livery to the long list.

During the autumn of 1987 Irish Continental Group (ICG) decided to launch itself on to the Smaller Companies' Market of the Stock Exchange. However, the collapse of international stock markets on Monday 19th October saw this deferred until 19th February 1988. The first day of dealing was 6th April, when IR£2.7 million was raised. As something like 80% of company employees subscribed to the issue, a significant proportion of the group's shareholding was in their hands. Business grew rapidly and in 1989 ICG raised further capital of IR£1.3 million under the Business Expansion scheme. Marine Investments of Luxembourg acquired a 20.7% stake.

In the same year ICG broadened its activities by taking a 50% shareholding in Eurocar Shipping, but after two years the venture proved unsuccessful so it withdrew, writing off the losses in the accounts for 1991.

Also in 1989 (November), Irish Ferries took Brittany Ferries' *Armorique* on charter for the Rosslare-Cherbourg and Le Havre crossings during the overhaul period. It was then chartered to Belfast Ferries to maintain the

Liverpool service while the S*aint Colum I* was off for overhaul.

By 1990 ICG achieved a turnover of IR£40 million and in the months November to March, outside the tourist season, the substantial freight and new car traffic accounted for virtually all business. To protect this valuable share of the market, and to cope with demand in the peak summer season, extra tonnage was chartered.

Business on the so-called Diagonal Corridor (between ports in Northern Ireland and north-west England) changed dramatically as newcomers started up rival freight services, prompting ICG to review its operations. Despite its modest success the Belfast-

Brittany Ferries *Armorique*; chartered by Irish Ferries in 1989. (FotoFlite)

NO TROUBLE IS TOO MUCH... NO DISTANCE IS TOO FAR

It was Christmas Eve and families all over the world were settling down to await the arrival of Santa Claus. Those travelling home from France to Ireland aboard the ferry *Saint Killian II* were no different.

With their cars safely tucked away on the car deck, Santa's precious cargoes onboard and all thoughts focused on a welcome homecoming, surely nothing could go wrong to spoil this idyllic moment?

Nothing... except the fire which was breaking out in the ship's engine room – a fire which would soon melt wires and immobilise the vessel's engines.

Immediately, emergency procedures were put into action at sea and ashore. Emergency services were alerted and the vessel was taken in tow to Falmouth port.

In parallel, a team at Head Office set to work, making arrangements to fly all of the passengers home to Ireland in time for Christmas dinner. An Aer Lingus jumbo jet was chartered, meaning its crew would have to interrupt their Christmas holiday to fly this mercy mission.

The same applied to staff at Dublin Airport so that the plane could land. Air traffic control personnel, baggage handlers and emergency teams all volunteered their time to be there on Christmas morning as the flight touched down.

In the midst of all this activity, an Irish Continental Line staffer thought, "What about Santa? How are all those children onboard our ship going to receive his Christmas gifts?"

And so another emergency measure was put in place – a volunteer appointed and appropriately kitted out with red costume and flowing white beard. A quick check of the ship's manifest revealed the numbers and ages of all children onboard.

Quickly, the statistics were sent to the toy departments at Arnotts and Clerys stores in Dublin and, in what seemed like an instant, Santa Claus was on his way by private plane so that he could be aboard the jumbo jet as it made its journey home. And in midflight, the jumbo's public address system cried the magic words "Ho ho ho!" and Santa emerged to greet an amazed, wide-eyed group of happy young boys and girls.

"And what's *your* age?" he asked each one in turn. And as the children answered, Santa and his helpers reached inside his sack and presented them with a surprise Christmas stocking filler.

In time, cars would be retrieved from the stricken vessel, which then lay tied up in Falmouth awaiting her journey to the repair yard. However, thanks to the quick thinking of ferry staff, every young child onboard that day discovered that there really *is* a Santa Claus, and that no distance can prevent him from bringing Christmas joy to boys and girls – even at 30,000 feet above the English countryside!

Maeve Barry, Hall Public Relations

Eamonn Rothwell (non Executive Director ICG); NCB Stockbrokers, Ken Beaton – President of the Irish Stock Exchange; and Paddy Murphy, Managing Director of ICG at the Irish Stock Exchange for the floatation of the company in 1988. (ICL)

Liverpool service was always problematic: a one-ship service with a punishing schedule of nightly sailings from Belfast and daytime returns from Liverpool, resulting all too frequently in mechanical problems for the *Saint Colum I*. Any unplanned withdrawal from service usually meant cancellation of the service. Passengers and freight drivers do not generally object to overnight crossings when comfortable cabins are available, but a tedious 9-hour daylight sailing is a different matter. Hence Belfast Ferries found itself needing a second ship to meet demand for night sailings in each direction, but not for the less popular day sailings. Possibilities for other daytime use included short runs to Scotland or the Isle of Man, but none could justify the investment or risk. In an ideal world the Belfast-Liverpool service would have been a two-ship operation, offering an overnight sailing from each port.

On 31st August 1990 it was announced that Belfast Ferries was to close. *Saint Colum I* made her final sailing from Belfast to Liverpool on the night of 14th October, under the command of Captain Jimmy Fullerton. After discharge at Liverpool she left the dock for the last time and was saluted by neighbouring ships. She returned to Belfast for removal of all stores and then set course for

Rosslare to undertake her final sailing for the company – to Le Havre with cargo.

Subsequently, the *Saint Colum I* was sold to Arkadia Line of Greece for its Igoumenitsa to Bari service under her new name – the *Dimitrios Express*. She arrived at Piraeus in December 1990 prior to a refit in Perama. Stability sponsons were added to her hull and her bow door was sealed. Passenger gangways were fitted either side of her stern ramp and her passenger accommodation was extended above bridge deck level. The Bari service closed in 1996, and she moved to Piraeus for further use, renamed *Poseidon Express 2*. Later owned by Hellas Ferries, and renamed yet again (as *Express Poseidon*), she still carried the shamrock of Irish Continental Line on her permanently-sealed bow visor – 27 years after being built. A fine vessel, she was finally sold to breakers in June 2005.

If the decision by ICG to close the Belfast-Liverpool service was perceived as negative in terms of the company's health, nothing could have been further from the truth. The acquisition of B&I Line just a year later was the first of several major advances which the future was to deliver.

Chapter eight

A New Force Afloat

For B&I Line more than for any other shipping company on the Irish Sea, the latter years of the 1980s were a time of great uncertainty, the tough challenges ahead compounded by the dire need for new tonnage – investment which the Irish Government, faced with cuts in national expenditure, would not sanction. And according to press reports at that time, B&I already had debts totalling IR£27 million.

It has to be said that misinformation and media speculation did not paint a rosy picture for B&I Line. Yet, at that time, the company was performing more than satisfactorily and was ahead of its budgeted trading profit. As Chief Executive Jim Kennedy pointed out in 1991, whilst acknowledging that there was still a long way to go, the plan of action introduced in 1988 was a five-year plan and, just 3 years on, the turnaround in B&I's fortunes was most encouraging.

But with no further Government investment forthcoming, and in line with what was happening in other parts of Europe, the scene was set for the company's privatisation, as had happened six years earlier to B&I Line's Irish Sea rival Sealink when sold off by the British Government.

Tenders for the purchase of B&I Line were received from P&O, Irish Continental Group plc and a consortium of B&I employees in conjunction with Maersk Line. In view of its long-standing links with B&I Line, P&O was considered to be the most likely buyer. However, by February 1991 the main contender was Irish Continental Group, and on 19th December the B&I Line Bill 1991 authorised sale of the company to ICG for IR£8.5 million, the Government also agreeing to write off past loans to B&I of IR£35 million.

The 1991 Bill was initiated in March 1990, when in addition to the Government debating the case for further Exchequer funding for B&I, the late Seamus Brennan, Minister for Tourism, Transport and Communications, announced his intention to review B&I's future options. His goal was to determine how soon the company's dependence on Exchequer support could be ended, taking into account the strategic shipping needs of importers, exporters and the tourism industry. To date the Exchequer had already injected IR£106 million into B&I, IR£53 million of which had been paid since 1985 as working capital. Yet not only was B&I still heavily dependent on the Exchequer but also seeking further major investment to replace and modernise the fleet.

Thus in August 1990 Seamus Brennan commissioned Stokes Kennedy Crowley Corporate

Finance Ltd (SKC) to advise him on the best and most economic means of terminating Exchequer support for B&I at the earliest possible time but without compromising passenger and freight shipping services to and from Ireland.

SKC examined the feasibility of four key options for B&I's future: continuation of the status quo; redevelopment through major capital investment; liquidation; the sale of the company. It concluded that the latter would produce the most favourable outcome, and the Government instructed SKC to explore how much interest the acquisition of B&I would generate in the international shipping market.

It quickly became apparent that there was no prospect of effecting a sale unless the Government agreed to take over the company's debt and there was a significant reduction in B&I's workforce. SKC also had discussions with the management of B&I, who had submitted a proposal for a staff/management buyout. SKC concluded that the Government should pursue the offer made by Irish Continental Group: it offered the best prospect of securing a strong, strategic shipping line, able to compete internationally and flying the Irish flag.

On the strength of SKC's recommendations, the Government decided (on 11th December 1990) against injecting further equity into B&I but to guarantee the minimum borrowing required to enable the company to continue trading thus avoiding liquidation, and on 16th January 1991 made the further decision to proceed with

negotiations for the sale of B&I to ICG. A Memorandum of Agreement (MoA) for the sale by the Minister for Finance of the entire share capital of B&I to ICG was signed on 28th February 1991. A clause in the agreement made provision that the agreement would lapse if, for whatever reason, the sale was not completed by 16th August 1991. Following the signing, ICG undertook a comprehensive due diligence exercise on B&I.

Prior to completion of the sale ICG also entered into extensive negotiations with the B&I unions to agree on rationalisation and work practices. However, this process took much longer than anticipated and by 16th August was still ongoing and the Memorandum of Agreement expired. Further detailed discussions continued and although progress was made, the expired MoA was not replaced by any new legal agreement.

During September the Chairman of B&I, acting on behalf of independent board directors, made it known to the Minister of Finance that in their view the terms of the proposed sale to ICG did not represent good value, and to achieve the best market price it was essential that competitive bids should be allowed and encouraged. At the same time a consortium of B&I management and staff, together with Danish backers, expressed its interest in acquiring the company and met with SKC to ask, inter alia, for permission to conduct its own due diligence exercise on B&I.

On 25th October both ICG and the B&I consortium were invited to submit their offers. These were assessed

The first AGM of ICG held in August 1988. From left to right: Eamon Rothwell, Terry Jones, Liam Booth, Captain Coleman Raftery, Tom Toner (Chairman), Patrick Murphy (MD), Frank Carey, John McGuckian and Alex Mullin. (ICG)

Ah, the history!

"It would be an impertinence to be too critical of the provisions in the Bill considering the agreement reached between all parties during the week. I do not think we can intervene in a harsh or a shrill way. The B&I Line is part of this country. It is part of my own experience. I go back nearly 40 years and I recall that as children we used to be taken to Sir John Rogerson's Quay and it was a great event of a summer's evening to watch the B&I boat going out. As a student, part of my experience was going to England to pick peas and we travelled on the old B&I boat. It was not all that comfortable.

"My most recent experience was when I was doing a charity walk for manic depression, for a group called ALONE, and we walked about 5 miles around Dublin. They provided us with a sheet of about 100 questions on old Dublin. Three weeks later I was telephoned to say I was the only one who got them all right! I had won first prize, which consisted of a return ticket for two on B&I to Liverpool. I was very surprised at the improvements which had been made. It had quite luxurious accommodation compared to what I remembered. The cabins were very comfortable with bunks and colour television and all the rest of it. There were facilities to make one's own coffee. It is a service that many Dubliners and people from the country will have used in various ways over many years and I will be sorry to see it disappear entirely.

"I welcome the involvement of Irish Continental Line. It is a strong, very professional group of companies. I have also had occasion to use its ferries. Senator Mooney rightly reminded us that we are, in fact, fast approaching a situation where we will be the only island nation in Europe and the implications of the Channel Tunnel are clearly there. However, curiously enough, we are not really a particularly maritime nation. We are aware of the fact that we are an island and are surrounded by the sea but the general attitude, far from having a real commitment to the role of the seafaring life in our nation, or to the importance of shipping or anything else, seems to be that echoed by Dominic Behan in his song which says:

The sea, oh the sea, is grá gheal mo chroí (bright love of my heart)
Long may it roll between England and me;
It's a sure guarantee that one day we'll be free,
Thank God we're surrounded by water."

Senator David Norris speaking on the sale of B&I Line

by a committee comprising representatives of the Ministry, the Department of Finance and SKC, and the unanimous recommendation was that the sale should be concluded with ICG subject to final agreement on all issues. The Government accepted the recommendation.

For the record, ICG's offer was IR£8.5m, coupled with a commitment to major investment in the short term and the consortium's was IR£5 million (of which 3 million was to be on a deferred basis) and both sought an Exchequer investment of IR£35 million prior to the sale to clear the company's debt.

Tourism, Transport and Communications Minister Seamus Brennan was satisfied that the sale to ICG represented the best way ahead for B&I. It would, he said, "create a strong shipping entity with substantial synergistic benefits, a proven track record and the ability to make the necessary future investment…over the next 5 years ICG is committed to investing more than £30 million in B&I."

Both the Irish Congress of Trade Unions and the B&I Group of Unions welcomed his views that the acquisition was in the best long-term interests of B&I, its employees and Ireland's shipping, tourism and export industries. However, ICG was under no illusion that B&I as it stood was an ineffective and inefficient drain on finances, and that archaic working practices which had endured for far too long were in drastic need of reform. This was borne out by the fact that even with the substantial 1988-90 job loses, costs rose by 11%. And poor service had seen customers voting by their absence

ICG's challenge was to rebuild the company and from the outset its stated intention was to keep it in Irish ownership. Plans and objectives for the 5 years ahead included the following major goals:

- Retention of all existing B&I shipping routes;
- Provision of extra capacity on the *Leinster*;
- Sourcing of an improved vessel to replace the *Munster* on the Rosslare-Pembroke Dock route;
- Upgrade of facilities throughout B&I;

Eamonn Rothwell

Taking over as ICG Chief Executive on the acquisition of B&I Line was true Dubliner Eamonn Rothwell, a non-executive director since 1987 when, through stockbrokers NCB, he advised on ICG's purchase of Irish Continental Line following the collapse of Irish Shipping.

A career in shipping had not been part of Eamonn's plans and his early working years were spent in accountancy. A Bachelor of Commerce, he next had a spell in financial journalism, employed briefly as a researcher for the now-defunct *Irish Business* magazine. It's possible that his time as a scribe is responsible for the fact that as one of Ireland's leading business people he prefers to stay out of the media spotlight, get on with the job and leave his numbers to do the talking.

From *Irish Business* Eamonn moved on to work for Bord Failte, the Irish Tourist Board, no doubt standing him in good stead for the future. He later managed equities in the US, UK, Japan and Europe for AIB (Allied Irish Banks). But it was his time as a director of NCB which forged the connection with Irish Continental.

Having been retained to manage the privatisation of Irish Continental Line, Eamonn involved a number of financial institutions before a floatation of the business in 1988. This was hotly followed by moves to privatise another Irish business, B&I Line, in 1992. It is a measure of the man that the B&I Line deal was closed on a Friday and on the following Monday he took over as Irish Continental's Managing Director. Never one to rest on his laurels, he immediately set his team to work on investing in new tonnage for the future.

While Eamonn Rothwell presided over the rescue of B&I Line's Irish Sea routes, in 2005 the groundswell of media opinion turned against him and the company when the fleet was flagged out and over 500 seafarers were replaced with agency staff. Although the majority of staff wanted the generous redundancy package, SIPTU (the trade union representing the ships' officers) came out against the offer.

The arrival of the agency crews led to a stand-off between management and officers, and gave rise to an intense political debate in Ireland. The dispute was ultimately resolved through the Irish Labour Relations Commission, but not before SIPTU conducted a long and bitter campaign seeking to force the company to reverse its decision – but it was not a decision taken lightly. In 2004 (the last full year before the company flagged out its crews) ICG's staff costs amounted to almost €68m. Compounded by continuing rises in fuel costs, a dip in profits was recorded.

By 2010 the roar of the Celtic Tiger economy had become a pitiful whimper. Having subjected ICG to a public flogging for bringing in agency crews, some elements of the Irish media were now conceding that the company, and Eamonn Rothwell in particular, had been wise to prepare the ground for the advance of the global financial crisis. ICG had defied the odds, delivering a 19% increase in profits for 2010 and reducing staff costs to €24m – a cut of almost 44m Euro, although fuel costs had risen by a further 10m Euro to €41.4m. These results were indisputable proof of the necessity and wisdom of Eamonn Rothwell's far-sighted and radical financial surgery; doing nothing was never an option for himself or his team of senior managers.

In 2013, as Ireland battles its way out of recession, the Irish ferry business still faces tough challenges and Irish Ferries is in very good shape to do so – alert to market sensitivities, steered by the firm and very dependable hand of Eamonn Rothwell, and on course to deliver ICG's commitment to enhancing B&I's customer service, providing long-term employment and ensuring a reasonable return to shareholders.

- Replacement of B&I's container ships;
- Provision of long term sustainable employment in B&I;
- Share ownership for B&I employees.

In snubbing the *Munster*, ICG made it abundantly clear that B&I's celebration of introducing such dilapidated tonnage to the Rosslare service had been a remarkable miscalculation! And the new owners of B&I wasted little time in embarking on a process of restructuring the company into three separate and distinct operating divisions, and introducing change wherever necessary to improve efficiency. Few of the existing senior management were retained and the need to cut costs resulted in many redundancies.

A NEW BROOM SWEEPS CLEAN

In the period between the passing of the legislation and the transfer of ownership, ICG actively sought a suitable replacement ship for the chartered *Munster*, and on 2nd January 1992 a three-year charter of the Stena AB vessel *Stena Nautica* was announced. Built for Danish State Railways at the Danish yard of Nakskov Shipsvaerf in 1986 as the *Niels Klim*, she operated the service between Aarhus and Kalundborg with her sister ship *Pedar Paars* until the link was discontinued in 1991 on the opening of the Great Belt Bridge. Both ships were acquired by Stena and renamed *Stena Nautica* and *Stena Invicta* respectively.

Following a competition across the UK travel trade, the ship was given the new name *Isle of Innisfree*, breaking the long tradition of naming B&I's main vessels after Ireland's provinces. She also introduced a new B&I Line livery. The band of three shades of blue at main deck level and rising aft to upper deck level was retained, but below this the hull was painted white with

The launch of Irish Ferries new electronic booking system for Freight, 1994. Left to right : Tony Kelly, Eamonn Rothwell, Brian Cowan TD (Minister for Transport), Michael Giblin, CCS Ltd. (irish Ferries)

red boot topping – very easy and pleasing on the eye. The company name and routes were still worn, but in blue on the white hull sides.

On 29th March 1992 the *Isle of Innisfree* (I) arrived at Rosslare from refit at Svendborg in Denmark under the command of Senior Master Captain Peter Ferguson. En route to Rosslare the ship called at Pembroke Dock for berthing trials in preparation for her entry into service on the 20.30 sailing to Pembroke Dock on 31st March. Meanwhile, the *Munster* completed her last sailing on the previous morning and was returned to her owners at Dublin Port. She spent almost a year awaiting sale, tied up on the River Liffey downstream of the East Link toll bridge. She later served as a cruise casino, initially in the Mediterranean and latterly off the Florida coast under the name *Ambassador II*.

In a display of B&I unity, the *Saint Killian II* was brought north to Dublin in March 1992, relieving the *Leinster* during her annual overhaul. When she returned to the Holyhead link, the *Leinster* too was showing off the new B&I Line colours – but under the new name of *Isle of Inishmore* (I), and her refit was to such a high standard that she received the Automobile Association's Most Improved Ferry Award. During the coming season the *Isle of Inishmore* (I) maintained the Dublin-Holyhead service.

No sooner had ICG taken charge at B&I than the company found itself embroiled in a complaint against Sealink to the European Commission over the abuse of a dominant position at Holyhead. In October 1991 Sealink, as Holyhead port authority, informed B&I that on 9th January 1992 it intended to introduce new sailing times. These would necessitate the movement of two

P&O's *Bison* in B&I colours for the Dublin-Liverpool ro-ro service. (Gordon Hislip collection)

ships past the B&I vessel while it was alongside the Admiralty Pier berth at Salt Island. At the time, Sealink and B&I occupied different berths at the port, Sealink using the prime Station Berth at the head of the harbour alongside the railway station. Due to the port's limitations, when a Sealink Stena vessel passed a moored B&I ship the water in the harbour rose and the ramp to the B&I ship had to be lifted for safety reasons, thereby interrupting loading.

Up until Sealink's proposed new sailing times, only one vessel (usually the *St Columba*, or *Stena Hibernia* as she was now known following Stena Line's purchase of the business) passed a B&I ferry while she was loading. But with the arrival of increased competition in the form of the *Stena Cambria*, Sealink Stena Line planned to have two ships passing during the B&I ferry's discharge and loading. B&I therefore requested the European Commission to adopt interim measures to prevent the implementation of Sealink Stena Line's new schedule, on the grounds that B&I services would be seriously disrupted due to the reduced time available in which to carry out these operations.

The Commission found that Sealink Stena Line had abused its dominant position, in breach of Article 86 of the EEC Treaty. In its capacity as port authority at Holyhead, Sealink Stena Line had permitted changes to its own ferry sailing times which could cause serious harm to B&I's loading and unloading procedures and

The chartered *Isle of Innisfree* alongside at Holyhead. (Miles Cowsill)

therefore its services, customer relations and commercial reputation. The Commission ordered interim measures against Sealink Stena Line which obliged it to alter some of its sailing times until the end of the summer season, or to return to its previous schedule, or to adopt any other schedule which did not lead to two vessels passing a B&I ferry during its loading or unloading. Sealink Stena Line was further instructed to comply within a month of this decision.

Meanwhile, at Rosslare, the *Isle of Innisfree* was proving very popular. However, her inability to maintain the schedule (4 hours 15 minutes in duration), particularly in bad weather, highlighted that she was not ideally suited to the demands of this Irish crossing and its exposure to prevailing south-westerly winds and Atlantic swells. As delivered, she was not fitted with fin stabilisers, making her 'uncomfortable' in heavy seas – a deficiency rectified during her spring 1993 dry docking – and she was moved to the Central Corridor (sea routes between Ireland, England and North Wales) Dublin-Holyhead service, swapping places with the *Isle of Inishmore*.

As the Salt Island berth at Holyhead was unsuitable for the *Isle of Innisfree*, Irish Ferries used the deep-water ro-ro berth in the outer harbour. A temporary terminal was provided by Stena Sealink Ports and linked to the berth by a very long covered walkway. This entailed foot passengers embarking and disembarking via the ship's vehicle deck, meaning that the unloading of vehicles was delayed until all foot passengers had left the vessel. Passage time between Dublin and Holyhead was extended from 3½ to 4 hours. During the last week of January 1994 the inevitable happened, the *Isle of Innisfree* damaging the berth when going alongside in a gale. She consequently returned to the Southern

Captain Peter Ferguson, Senior Master of Irish Ferries until retirement in 2001. (ICL)

IRISH FERRIES An Ambitious Voyage

The renamed *Leinster*; the *Isle of Inishmore* arrives at Pembroke Dock with Neyland town behind. (Miles Cowsill)

Corridor and the *Isle of Inishmore* returned to Holyhead, sailing to the Admiralty Pier.

With traffic increasing steadily, the Irish Continental Group considered all tonnage options, including the possibility of extending the *Leinster* to increase capacity. Investment in a new purpose-built ship became increasingly tempting, and negotiations were initiated with several shipyards. In 1993 ICG took the big step: placing an order with Samsung Heavy Industries in South Korea. On the eve of signing a contract, ICG was then shocked when SHI pulled out owing to lack of experience in building ro-pax vessels. ICG turned next to Van der Giessen-de-Noord of Krimpen, Rotterdam, for a 23,000 tonne vessel, at a cost of IR£46 million. This was to be the first Irish-flagged passenger ship to be built since the *Leinster*. Options were also taken to purchase other vessels from the Dutch yard at guaranteed prices. The hull for the new ship was based on the tried and tested Van der Giessen-built *Norbank* and *Norbay* (late 1993 and early 1994 respectively), then operated by P&O North Sea Ferries on its Hull-Europoort route (and latterly operated out of Dublin).

The transformation of a troubled state shipping line to a strong and profitable private company was underway, the activities of 1995 providing ample

illustration. From 1st January 1995 the trading name for all Irish Continental Group's services became Irish Ferries. The venerable 160-year-old name British and Irish Steam Packet Company, linked during 1993 and 1994 with its new parent company as 'B&I Line – an Irish Ferries Company' – disappeared almost without a whimper.

ENTER THE *ISLE OF INNISFREE*

The new Holyhead vessel was launched four weeks later, on 27th January, by Clodagh Moreland, wife of ICG Chief Executive Eamonn Rothwell. The *Isle of Innisfree* (II) carried Irish Ferries' new livery: white hull with green boot topping, the company name on her superstructure and, aft, a large stylised motif in the company colours of green, light blue and dark blue. The funnel was as before – green, the company flag superimposed, and topped off in black.

The *Isle of Innisfree* (I) left Dublin for the last time in February, serving the final weeks of her charter at Rosslare. She was replaced on the Holyhead run by the versatile *Saint Patrick II*, which in turn made way for the *Isle of Inishmore* pending the arrival of the new ship. On its return to Stena, the *Isle of Innisfree* (I) was refitted for service with Lion Ferries on the Grenaa to Verberg

The *Isle of Innisfree* arriving at Pembroke Dock. (Miles Cowsill)

and Halmstad routes and renamed *Lion King*. She remains in service as the *Stena Nautica*.

The *Isle of Innisfree* (II) arrived in Dublin on 15th May 1995, under the command of her newly-appointed Senior Master, Captain Peter Ferguson, and took up service eight days later. She was an instant success – reliable and well patronised from the start.

Her outstanding interior decor and comfort were a huge advance on anything seen before, and public areas were light, airy and beautifully designed, featuring stylish curves in materials which complemented each other with striking effect: marble, wood (burnished and polished), glass (engraved and smoked), and stainless steel.

Backing the entrance hall was a mirror rising two decks high and depicting a flight of birds in bronze. Aft of the superstructure, the huge windows of the two-tier panoramic lounge gave sea views over the stern and to both sides. Onboard facilities all bore names associated with Irish poet William Butler Yeats, whose work *The Lake Isle of Innisfree* was also the inspiration for the ship's name. And her entry into service not only introduced and firmly established the cruiseferry concept on the Irish Sea – it also heralded a steady and very welcome increase in market share for Irish Ferries.

In the face of competition from Stena Line, the new *Isle of Innisfree* became a watchword for comfort and reliability. Despite the occasional horrendous weather conditions she missed very few sailings on the Holyhead route, and in summer 1996 was so well patronised that Irish Ferries had to charter the *Purbeck* from Sally Line to cope with overflow freight traffic.

In fact, Ireland's economic boom was driving freight

At the renaming of the *Isle of Inishmore* (1), 1992 : Frank Carey, Marketing Director, Austin Conboy (Euroshipping), Alex Mullin, Operations Director, Austin Cody, On Board Services Manager.

business to an unprecedented high, and on the Southern Corridor route the *Isle of Inishmore* (I), in new Irish Ferries colours, was struggling to meet demand too (both passenger and freight) and the need to replace her with a bigger ship was now more urgent. Remarkably, the new *Isle of Innisfree* too was already working to capacity, and Irish Ferries began grappling with the idea of building an even bigger new ship for Dublin, and at Rosslare replacing the *Isle of Inishmore* (I) with the *Isle of Innisfree*.

The company approached shipyards in Germany, Norway, Finland, Italy and, once again, Korea, but it was the Dutch yard of Van der Giessen-de-Noord at Rotterdam that won the day. On 4th October 1996 a second and larger new vessel for Irish Ferries was launched by Sandra Carey, wife of Frank Carey, then the company's Marketing Director.

The new ship, *Isle of Inishmore* (II), was constructed to the builder's tried and tested hull design, as employed in the then-recent *Stena Jutlandica* for Stena Line's Gothenburg–Frederikshavn service. Enhanced to meet the more demanding conditions of the Irish Sea, the new ship represented an investment of IR£60 million and after launch was moved to a fitting-out berth on the River Maas. The weather in northern Europe in October and November 1996 was unusually stormy, and on one such occasion the *Isle of Inishmore* slipped her moorings and drifted, coming to rest on the riverbank at the rear of a local resident's garden. It was said that he called the yard to ask if the large white and green ship in his garden was anything to do with them! She sustained slight damage to her port rudder and propeller, but fortunately her engines were not coupled to the shafts. She also narrowly escaped contact with a

Flowers are presented by a Dutch schoolgirl to the Godmother of the *Isle of Innisfree*, Clodagh Moreland. (Irish Ferries)

road over-bridge and potentially disastrous consequences.

Despite this little adventure the new ship was just a few days late in being handed over to her owners and Irish Ferries made no issue of it, considering the matter to be nothing more than an unfortunate incident. So the company was completely taken aback when, in a display of true professionalism and integrity, the yard raised the matter of compensation, which Irish Ferries gratefully accepted in the form of an attractive addition to the ship – the Dun Aengus sky lounge. Sky lounges were a popular feature of the first car ferries *Leinster* and *Innisfallen*. The only indication that it was a late addition to the ship was the lack of a lift all the way up to Deck 11!

Shortly after 10.30 on 17th February 1997, the new *Isle of Inishmore* – then the largest passenger-car ferry

An aft view of the construction of the *Isle of Innisfree* at Van der Giessen de Nord in March 1995. (Irish Ferries)

Freight boom! The chartered *Purbeck* arrives at Dublin from Holyhead. (Gordon Hislip)

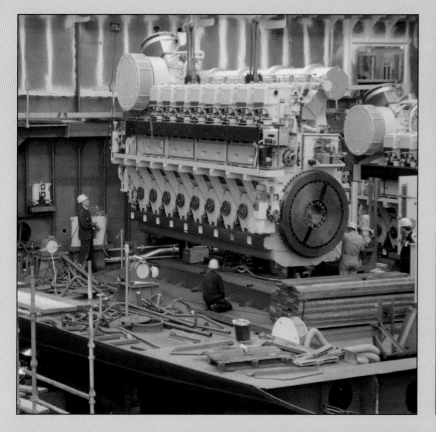

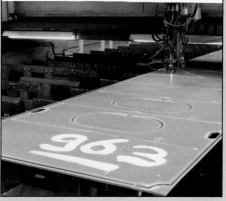

Top left: The port main engine placed on block 208 in September 1994. (Irish Ferries)

Top right: Cutting of the first plate of the *Isle of Innisfree* after the signing of the contract between both parties. (Irish Ferries)

Left: The bow visor is moved into position on the *Isle of Innisfree*. (Irish Ferries)

Above: This view shows the erected hull of the *Isle of Innisfree* during December 1994 with the erection of the wheelhouse in progress. (Irish Ferries)

in north-west Europe – arrived in Dublin from Rotterdam in gale force conditions with Captain Peter Ferguson in command. She then spent almost two weeks berthed at various locations within the port, open to invited guests, and completing berthing trials both here and at Holyhead, entering service on the morning of 2nd March as the largest ship thus far to sail under the Irish flag.

On 22nd March 1997 the former *Leinster* , renamed *Isle of Inishmore* (1) (renamed again as *Isle of Inishturk* in 1996 to release her name for the yet-to-be built new *Isle of Inishmore*) was replaced on the Rosslare-Pembroke Dock route by the *Isle of Innisfree* (II), although as facilities at Pembroke Dock were not ready in time she initially sailed to and from Fishguard. The faithful servant then sailed for lay-up at Le Havre pending sale and was purchased in June 1997 by the Canadian Government. She was renamed *Madeleine* for the CTMA service between Prince Edward Island and the Magdalen Islands.

At the time of placing the order in 1993 for the *Isle of Innisfree* (II), plans were put in hand for new terminal facilities at both Dublin and Holyhead, the latter necessitating the construction of a new berth. Holyhead's first so-called double-deck ferry entered service for Sealink in 1981, but there were no double-deck links shoreside to achieve rapid turnaround of vessels by means of simultaneous discharge and loading. To accommodate Irish Ferries, double-deck vehicle-loading ramps were provided at both termini – the first at ports in Wales and the Republic of Ireland. The Holyhead facility came into use in late 1995, prior to which the *Isle of Innisfree* continued to use the outer deep-water berth, with much inconvenience to foot

Hugh Coveney, TD Minister for Marine during a visit to *Isle of Innisfree* in 1995. Also pictured with him is Captain Jack Duignan, Eamonn Gilmore TD, Minister of State, Dept of Marine and Tom Toner, Chairman ICG. (Irish Ferries)

passengers. Although relatively new, this berth was a long way behind contemporary standards and its approach from seaward also left a lot to be desired. Naturally, with the transfer of the *Isle of Innisfree* to Rosslare, double-deck facilities were required there and at Pembroke Dock.

An interesting exercise in December 1995 was the operation of the *Saint Killian II* on a round trip between Dublin and Liverpool for fans travelling to a Holland-Ireland football match. Leaving Dublin at 07.45, the ship was alongside Liverpool's Pier Head by 15.00, the return sailing departing at 23.59. But the initiative was poorly supported and a proposed repeat performance abandoned.

FAST-FERRY ERA

The 1992 arrival into service of a fast ferry between Northern Ireland and Scotland heralded the first high-speed car ferry in Irish waters. Sea Containers had previously attempted to introduce its SeaCat on a new service from Holyhead to Dun Laoghaire but had been unable to secure berthing slots at the Welsh port. The craft was instead introduced between Belfast and Stranraer to immediate success. The concept delivered new reasons to travel by sea and faster crossings opened up new markets, particularly in the day-trip and short-break sector.

The drawback was that in poor weather conditions, where no back-up vessel was available, cancelled sailings were inevitable. Yet there was still something of a frenzy as operators beat a path to builders in a clamour to enter the fast-ferry arena and, on the Irish Sea, catamarans, monohulls and semi-swath fastcraft

Tom Toner and Mr & Mrs Eamonn Rothwell are welcomed by Mr & Mrs Timmers of Van der Giessen de Nord. (Irish Ferries)

The *Isle of Innisfree* on sea trials on a benign North Sea in 1995. (FotoFlite)

Looking smart in her new Irish Ferries colours, the first *Isle of Inishmore*. (Miles Cowsill)

were proof that a market was here to be exploited.

Irish Ferries monitored this enterprise with great interest, in particular the progress in technical developments in design, construction and operation, and the company was in no doubt that to maintain its market sector it needed to compete. Led by Eamonn Rothwell, the team of Alex Mullin, Captain Eddie Keane, John Reilly and Tony Kelly concluded that the best solution to cater for Irish Sea conditions and poor weather was a combination of a fast ferry backed up by a reliable cruiseferry. They were in no doubt that such a service would bring benefits, not least an increase in the number of round trips per day offered to customers – a choice of six compared with two.

By 1998, following discussions with Incat Tasmania – builders of several fastcraft then operating on the Irish Sea – it was time to make a move. The Western Australian shipbuilder Austal Ships Pty was also engaged in discussions with Irish Ferries. In June of that year, ICG announced placing an order for a purpose-built twin-hulled Austal Auto Express 86-metre fastcraft capable of maintaining 39 knots. In construction, with the Irish Sea in mind, Austal paid particular attention to strengthening around the bow area. As for passenger areas, Irish Ferries' fit out style created a truly relaxed environment

in what had become a pretty functional norm in the high speed ferry sector.

The order value was IR£25 million, bringing the company's investment in new tonnage over a 4-year period to IR£230 million. Delivery was scheduled for early 1999, in time for the summer peak season. Fittingly named *Jonathan Swift* and marketed under the brand DUBLIN*Swift*, the striking new vessel commenced her long delivery voyage to Dublin from Fremantle, via Piraeus, on 11th April 1999, commanded by Captains Steve Hutson, Tony Canavan and Paul Devaney. On the first leg she called into Xilacap in Indonesia, Cochin on the western seaboard of India, and Djibouti at the southern entrance of the Red Sea. At each port fresh water, fuel and stores were taken onboard. After passing through the Suez Canal she arrived in Piraeus to undertake demonstration sailings on behalf of her builders. The *Jonathan Swift* next called into Gibraltar, arriving in Dublin on 5th June 1999 – the end of a voyage of 10,354 nautical miles. Her progress en route was charted by a dedicated website – a hugely successful marketing initiative. The captains posted their daily onboard log, and there was a facility for schools to email the ship direct. There was also a competition to win a holiday worth £2,000.

Irish Ferries ordered the *Isle of Inishmore* from Van der Giessen de Nord in 1996. The vessel was constructed by the Dutch company and delivered to Irish Ferries in 14 months. The views on this page show the various stages of construction of the ship which could accommodate 802 cars and 2,200 passengers. (Ferry Publications Library Photos)

Isle of Innismore

Top left: Reception Area
Left: Kilronan Motorist's Club
Top right: Boylan's Brasserie
Middle right: Reception Area
Top right: Club Class Lounge

The *Isle of Inishmore* entered commercial service between Dublin and Holyhead on 2nd March 1997. (FotoFlite)

The new DUBLIN*Swift* service was due to commence on 15th June, following crew training, familiarisation, berthing trials and emergency evacuation exercises. The excitement of the fastcraft's introduction was somewhat tempered though when some of the restrictive practices of the old B&I Line days raised their heads, resulting in her debut being delayed by an industrial dispute between Irish Ferries and the trade union SIPTU, which represented seven officers transferred from the company's conventional ferry operations to man the new high-speed craft. The officers' grievance was the manning levels proposed by Irish Ferries – lower than for the fleet's conventional ferries. Irish Ferries responded quickly, and the threat was real: the new vessel would be sold or chartered if the issue was not resolved. Consequently, it was not until 3rd July that the first revenue-earning sailing was made – the 12.15 departure for Holyhead under the command of Captain Colm Clare.

THE WORLD'S BIGGEST FERRY

On 8th July 1999, just days after the *Jonathan Swift*'s

Irish Ferries' 1997 Irish Sea fleet, the *Isle of Inishmore* and the *Isle of Innisfree*. (Irish Ferries)

This view shows the wealth of freight space on the upper deck of the *Isle of Inishmore*. At both Pembroke Dock and Rosslare the ship loads using a twin decked linkspan. (FotoFlite)

maiden voyage, ICG announced yet another newbuild. With freight traffic continuing to grow, the *Isle of Inishmore* quickly – and unpredictably – proved too small to cope with demand. ICG had considered introducing a second ro-ro ship to assist her, but this was ruled out on the grounds that it would be uneconomic. This raised the possibility of another, even larger, new ship to replace the *Isle of Inishmore*; greater economies of scale meant that such a ship made sense, but there was a problem of sheer size and the operational confines of both Dublin and Holyhead. Operations Director John Reilly and Shipping Business Director Captain Eddie Keane set to work on a solution. If port confines limited and dictated a ship's length, there was only one way to go – up!

The new ship – all 12 decks of her – was ordered from Aker Finnyards Oy of Rauma, Finland, at a cost of IR£80 (€100million). Based on vehicle deck capacity (as opposed to gross tonnage), she was to be the world's largest passenger and vehicle ferry, bringing ICG's investment in new tonnage up to a mammoth €457 million. Other vital statistics included an overall length of 209.02 metres, a breadth of 31.8 metres, the depth to main deck 9.9 metres, a moulded depth of 15.75

metres, and a draught of 6.4 metres.

A competition to name her, open to all, came up trumps – *Ulysses*, not only the Roman name for Odysseus, the hero of Greek mythology who undertook epic sea voyages, but also the title of one of the best-known works of Dublin-born writer James Joyce. The

At the naming ceremony of the *Jonathan Swift* in 1999, Tom Toner, Chairman ICG, Bertie Ahern TD, Taoiseach (Prime Minister), Captain Steve Hutson, Ms Celia Larkin (Godmother). (Irish Ferries)

keel of the *Ulysses* was laid on 24th January 2000, and on 1st September the part-completed vessel was floated out of Aker Finnyard's facility.

THE END OF DUTY-FREE

In the first year of the new millennium, things continued to go reasonably well for Irish Ferries, despite the ending of duty-free sales on 30th June 1999.

The abolition of the duty-free concession for passengers travelling between EU member states certainly posed a hefty new challenge for all sea and air operators. As an island nation Ireland was particularly hard hit, revenue from onboard passenger spend traditionally subsidising cheap access. A report by the European Travel Research Foundation had warned that around 50,000 jobs would be lost in ferry and related tourism industries. The report also suggested that ferry services across the Dover Straits between the UK and the Continent would be almost halved in number, and that fares on those routes which remained would rise by at least 10%, with similar increases in Ireland – the only EU country with no land link to the rest of Europe. The report went even further in its condemnation of the abolition of duty-free sales, suggesting that it would probably result in the closure of all of Ireland's direct ferry services to Continental Europe, resulting in much

The *Jonathan Swift* under construction at Austal's Fremantle yard in 1998. (Irish Ferries)

The *Jonathan Swift* pulls away from Dublin on her early morning sailing to Anglesey. (Gordon Hislip)

The *Jonathan Swift* swinging off the linkspan at Holyhead. (Miles Cowsill)

longer road journeys through Ireland, the UK and France.

Despite pleas from industry, the EU Commission recommended no deferral of the duty-free abolition deadline. Public Enterprise Minister Mary O'Rourke, who led Ireland's campaign to keep duty-free, responded: "I imagine the European heads of state will have a lot to say about this. Who rules Europe? Is it the elected heads of government or the unelected commission?"

However, in the 12 months beginning 1st July 1999 – the first full year in which the effect of the abolition of duty-free could be gauged – the number of passengers carried by Irish Ferries hit a new record of 1.8 million, an overall growth of 6.7%. This was a creditable performance given that P&O Irish Sea had commenced carrying passengers from Dublin and Merchant Ferries had introduced two large multi-purpose vessels, also operating from Dublin. On Irish Ferries' Dublin-Holyhead route, including the full-year benefit of the

fast-ferry service, passenger numbers increased by 14% to 1.15 million. And although the Rosslare-Pembroke route experienced an 8.1% decline in passengers (to 450,000), car numbers increased. The Ireland-France service saw passenger numbers grow by 5.7% to 207,000.

However, the combination of the abolition of duty-free sales and the sustained increase in fuel prices substantially affected costs and reduced margins, the company recording a decline in profits. To remain healthy, and to avoid the pitfalls which had turned B&I into a cumbersome and inefficient leviathian, ICG needed to find ways in which to make cutbacks. The immediate plan was to promote the charter of either the *Isle of Inishmore* or the *Isle of Innisfree* pending entry into service of the *Ulysses*.

THE *ULYSSES* TAKES HER BOW

The *Ulysses* was handed over to ICG at Rauma on 22nd February 2001 and sailed under the command of Captain Peter Ferguson (delivering his 4th vessel for the company), at 07.40 on 28th February, arriving in Dublin Bay at 07.00 on Sunday 4th March. Watched by hundreds of onlookers on the South Great Wall of Dublin Port, the

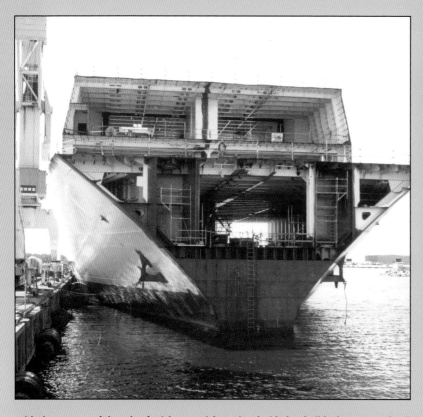

With the success of the *Isle of Inishmore* Irish Ferries decided to build what was at the time the world's largest ferry for the Dublin-Holyhead service. Aker Finnyards won the contract to build the ship, which was built at Rauma. The vessel was constructed in a dry dock and then floated out.

Top left: This view shows the vessel under construction and clearly shows the large car/freight decks which were to be the overwhelming success of the ship's pedigree.

Top right: The funnel of the *Ulysses* being placed in position at the yard.

Above: Eamonn Rothwell, with the Manager of Finnyards, opens the release valves to allow the *Ulysses* to float out of her dry dock.

Below: The *Ulysses* shortly before being floated out at Finnyards.

(Irish Ferries/Ferry Publications Library)

Welcome to Dublin! The *Ulysses* arrives at Dublin for the first time, greeted by a Dublin Port tug and the outward *Jonathan Swift*. February 2001. (Irish Ferries)

Ulysses passed the Poolbeg Light just before midday. She tied up at Berth 49 at 12.26, following the *Jonathan Swift*'s 12.15 sailing to Holyhead, the two vessels having crossed in the River Liffey. The *Ulysses* vacated the berth at about 14.00 to facilitate the arrival of Sea Container's fastcraft *Rapide* and turned in the river before running astern to tie up at a South Quay berth.

After a period of crew training, MES drills and berthing trials at both Dublin and Holyhead, the new vessel was blessed on 21st March and named *Ulysses* by her 'Godmother' Mairéad Berry, the Irish Paralympic Gold Medal-winning swimmer. On the ship's maiden voyage on 25th March, under the command of Captain Tom Joyce, she left for Holyhead at 12.15.

The *Ulysses* has seating for up to 1,938 passengers, an alternative configuration offering 117 twin or single cabins accommodating up to 228 passengers. Her impressive amenities include a pub, various lounges – notably Leopold Bloom's main lounge and the panoramic sky/Martello observation lounge on Deck 11 – as well as restaurants and the Grafton shopping area. In keeping with the Ulysses theme are the Nora Barnacle's food emporium and the Volta twin-screen cinema. There is also a gaming area and the Quays

Mairead Berry, Irish Paralympic Swimming Champion and Godmother of the *Ulysses* with Captain Peter Ferguson after naming ceremony, 2001. (Irish Ferries)

Restaurant. Freight drivers have their own dedicated club lounge and restaurant, and the 83 cabins for officers and crew on Decks 10 and 11 provide 121 berths.

Vehicle deck capacity totals 4,080 lane metres, capable of taking up to 1,300 cars or 260 articulated truck and trailer units, or a practical combination of both. Significantly, the vehicle deck capacity is arranged on four fixed decks, the 4th of which introduces a new feature for RoPax ferries. In designing the *Ulysses*, turnaround times were a crucial consideration and the desired efficiency was achieved by drive-through on two levels facilitated by separate bow and stern access arrangements for the main and upper freight decks. Based on a comprehensive shipboard RoRo access/internal transfer outfit from MacGREGOR, this comprised the following features:

- 2 axial stern ramp/doors, arranged port and starboard on the main deck reaching on to the linkspan. Each has a length of 8 metres (+ 2 metre end flaps) and offers a driveway of 9.7 metres/10.2 metres on to the main trailer deck (3) via a 10.1 metre wide x 5.2 metres high clear opening.
- Bow door, in 2 sections, yielding a clear opening 7.0 metres wide x 6 metres high into Deck 3.

- Bow ramp, in 3 sections, with an overall length of 20 metres (+ 2-metre end flaps) and offering a 6-metre driveway into a clear opening 6 metres wide x 5.2 metres high on Deck 3.
- Ramp cover, side-hinged and watertight, arranged near midships on the starboard side of Deck 3 over a fixed ramp leading to the tanktop cargo hold. The 2-section cover, 48 metres long x 4.8 metres wide, offers a clear opening breadth of 4.4 metres. Automated handrails are included on one side of the hatch end.
- Hoistable tilting ramp, serving between main and upper trailer decks, arranged to port of the centreline. The 48 metres long (+2.6 metres end flaps) ramp offers a driveway of 3.1 metres and a clear opening 3.2 metres wide x 5 metres high.
- Hoistable tilting ramp, serving between upper (5) and top (7) trailer decks, arranged midships on the starboard side. The 48 metres long (+ 2.6 metres end flaps) ramp offers a driveway of 4.8 metres and a clear opening 5 metres wide x 5 metres high. (Both hoistable tilting ramps can be lowered at either end by disconnectable hinges forward and aft. In the raised position

The impressive *Ulysses* arriving off the Welsh coast. (Ronald Roberts)

they form a weathertight closure in the associated deck.)

● Hoistable car decks, arranged between the top trailer deck (7) and the public deck, running port and starboard. The 64-metre-long decks are formed by 6 panels (3 port and starboard), with access at each end provided by 19.4 metres-long (+ 2 metre end flaps) hoistable ramps; hoisting is performed by jigger winches located within the deck panels. In the lowered

(7). The side-hinged door, located on the curved fixed ramp on the port side leading from Deck 5 to Deck 7, provides a clear opening 3.5 metres wide x 3.5 metres high.

● 3 top-hinged passenger doors (1 to port and 2 to starboard), each offering a clear opening 2 metres wide x 2.2 metres high to Deck 7.

With a reputation for reliability, even in the worst of Irish Sea conditions, Irish Ferries was careful to ensure

Club Class Lounge - *Ulysses* (Maritime Photographic)

(working) position the decks offer clear heights below/above of 2.8 metres/2.1 metres; stowed, they provide a clear height below of 5 metres. Handrails at the sides of car decks and ramps are deployed automatically.

● Top-hinged front door allowing vehicle traffic to access the open garage on the upper trailer deck (5) via a 6 metres wide x 5.1 metres high opening.

● Upper front door allowing passenger cars to access the open garage on the top trailer deck

that this much larger ship would not come at the expense of operating performance. A service speed of 22 knots at 85% maximum continuous rating was specified, power provided by 4 MaK M43 medium-speed diesel engines arranged in pairs. Each 9-cylinder 430mm-bore model delivers 7,800kW at 500rpm, giving a total of 31,200kW. These engine pairs are linked to a gearbox, which reduces speed to 144.4rpm. This gearbox is in turn connected by shafts to a 5.1-metre diameter LIPS type 4CI6 CP propeller with 4 high-skew blades.

Each gearbox also drives two shaft alternators at

Ulysses

Top left: Leopard Blooms Bar
Left: Café Lafayette
Top right: Main car deck
Middle right: Reception Area
Top right: Café Lafayette

All photos Maritime Photographic

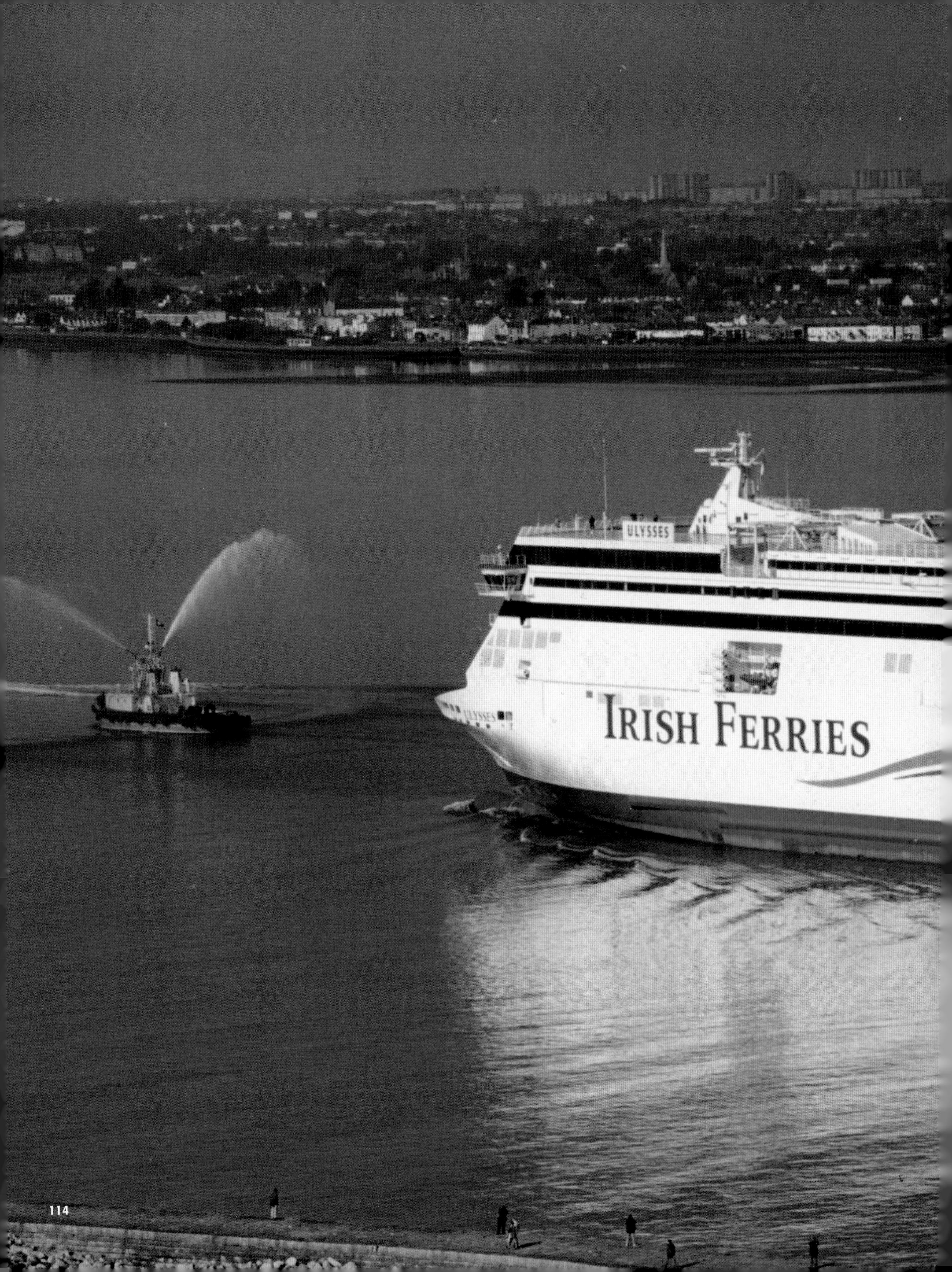
ULYSSES
IRISH FERRIES

The *Ulysses* slowly manoeuvres her way along the Channel to Dublin port on 28th February 2001 with the suburb of Clontarf in the backgroound. (Irish Ferries)

The *Isle of Inishmore* swings off the berth at Pembroke Dock.
(Miles Cowsill)

Eugene Carron, Freight Manager with Master of the *Ulysses*,
Captain Tom Joyce, cutting 1st Birthday Cake in 2002. (Irish Ferries)

1,500rpm. These 4 units (each 3,100kVA) supply power
at sea; however, there are also 3 1,520kW gensets based
on MaK 8M20 engines running at 1,000rpm. Electricity
at 6.6V is generated by Leroy Somer alternators via a
Semco Maritime switchboard.

Importantly, three bow thrusters and 1 stern thruster
assist manoeuvring. All are LIPS type CT 275 transverse
units, rated at 2,400kW with a 2.75m propeller. Steering
is enabled by 2 Beker FKSR flap rudders, each with a
surface area of 16.4m² and operated by Porsgrunn
electro-hydraulic rotary vane steering gear, giving a 65°
angle each side. Anchor and mooring is carried out
using a Rauma Brattvaag AC-electric deck gear outfit
from Rolls Royce.

The introduction of the *Ulysses* doubled Irish Ferries'
capacity on the Dublin-Holyhead route and released the
Isle of Inishmore to transfer to the Rosslare-Pembroke
Dock service, just 4 years after her maiden voyage, and
in turn made the *Isle of Innisfree* available for charter to
P&O Ferries at Portsmouth.

The *Ulysses* won the Lloyds List Cruise + Ferry 2001
award in the category 'Most significant newbuild – Ferry'
for Irish Continental Group and her builders. It was
particularly unfortunate that the introduction of the
vessel coincided with the outbreak in the UK of Foot
and Mouth disease and the attendant travel restrictions,
both voluntary and otherwise. Schedules were thrown
into chaos as disinfection precautions had to be taken at
ports. This was followed by the significant increase in
the price of oil and a consequent fall in profits for 2000
– and all exacerbated by the abolition of duty-free
concessions. The economies of scale of Irish Ferries'

operations equipped the company to ride the storm of
further recession (rather better than its competitors did)
which followed the atrocity of the terrorist attacks on the
Pentagon in Washington and World Trade Centre in New
York on 11th September 2001.

In the face of stiff competition, and adverse trading
conditions in general, not only did Irish Ferries maintain
its overall trading performance in 2001 – it also won the
Best Ferry Company Award from the Irish travel trade for
the 5th year in succession.

Throughout the pressures which mounted on Irish
Ferries, the combination of the *Ulysses* and the
Jonathan Swift proved to be highly successful, the
fastcraft reliable in all but the worst sea conditions and
praised by passengers. But there was a down side – in
April 2002 the *Jonathan Swift* attracted attention of a
different kind, Stena Line taking legal action against Irish
Ferries in London's High Court on the basis that the
fastcraft's design infringed Stena Line's patent for
'Superstructure for Multi-hull Vessels;' European Patent
(UK) No. 0 648 173, which related to the design of the
vessel such that stability is enhanced by prevention of
'hogging' and 'sagging' in the hulls. Stena's claim to
patent was upheld by Mr Justice Laddle, but the
infringement was not allowed on the basis that the
vessel was 'temporarily or accidentally' in UK internal or
territorial waters.

The maximum time which the vessel (which is
registered and based in Dublin) spends at any one time
in UK waters, weather permitting, is 3 hours. This fact
enabled the *Jonathan Swift* to take advantage of the 'get
out clause' in the Patents Act. The fact that the vessel

makes 3 to 4 crossings per day emphasises the temporary nature of its entry, as well as the fact that it is being used in the international carriage of goods and passengers. Accordingly, while Stena's claim to its patent was sustained, Irish Ferries succeeded on the basis of defending the claim for infringement. In February 2003 Stena appealed the judgement but without success. A subsequent appeal to the House of Lords by Stena also failed to have the earlier judgement overturned. However, in October 2003, agreement was reached between Stena and Austal Ships that Austal would pay royalties to Stena in respect of any craft constructed using the method which was the subject of their patent. For their part Stena undertook to discontinue any action against all operators of the Austal-built craft concerned.

On 25th March 2002 the *Ulysses* marked the first anniversary of her maiden voyage, with the proud record of never having missed a single sailing and completing 1,395 voyages, covering some 76,725 nautical miles in the process. This evidence of her reliability was capitalised upon by freight operators, which in turn led to a 13% growth in business during a year which was blighted by the fallout from Foot and Mouth disease. It

all added up to a unique achievement for her owners, establishing Irish Ferries as leading operator sailing from the port of Holyhead.

On Sunday 23rd February the *Ulysses* collided with, and damaged, a mooring dolphin and the passenger gangway while berthing in difficult conditions at Holyhead, resulting in cancellation of her service to and from the Welsh port for a number of days. Her sailings were covered by the fastcraft *Jonathan Swift*, running to a revised timetable. In the meantime, between 25th and 28th February, Irish Ferries' freight sailings to and from Dublin were operated by the *Ulysses* using the Twelve Quays river berth at Birkenhead.

Business in 2003 was most challenging, especially with the introduction of new tonnage by competitors, most recently in the form of the *Stena Adventurer*, marketed as the longest (but not the largest) ferry operating on the Irish Sea. The Irish Travel Trade award for Best Ferry Company in 2003 went to Irish Ferries for a record seventh year.

The *Isle of Innisfree* is seen here inward bound during her last few weeks in service on the Rosslare-Pembroke Dock route. (Miles Cowsill)

Chapter nine

Looking to France

While ICG revamped the former B&I routes, the future of the French routes, which were the backbone of ICG's activity, was always in mind, especially replacement of the *Saint Killian II* and *Saint Patrick II* – ships which were then almost 20 years old and unsuited to competing successfully in the 1990s. On 1st November 1993 the company took industry observers completely by surprise by stating its intentions and its commitment to the future of the Ireland-France segment of ICG's by then expanding activity

In 1994 Irish Ferries announced a new route to the Breton port of Brest – a shorter crossing than to Cherbourg or Le Havre. But in delaying authorisation for construction of the necessary linkspan, the French authorities effectively blocked this venture and ICG complained to the EU Competition Commissioner before turning its attention to an alternative destination – Roscoff.

Here too there was a problem – an objection by Morlaix Chamber of Commerce, the port authority. Mindful of its previous experiences with Stena Ports at Holyhead, Irish Ferries stated its case to Karel van Miert (EU Competition Commissioner) on the basis that the port operators were trying to preserve the monopoly held by Brittany Ferries on its route to and from Cork. Morlaix Chamber of Commerce argued that Irish Ferries had published service schedules without having first agreed time slots with the port. The Commissioner came down on the side of Irish Ferries and services commenced in 1994 with the 08.30 arrival of the *Saint Patrick II* at Roscoff on 16th June – sixteen days later than first planned.

Disappointingly, tourist numbers to and from France in the high seasons of 1995 and 1996 fell some way below expectations. Coupled with the loss of a contract to deliver new cars (an important subsidy in part for winter services), it led the company to apply to the Irish Government for a subvention in order to maintain all-year-round services on French routes, based on the precedent of support from the French Government for Brittany Ferries. The application, to Sean Barrett T.D., Minister for Defence and the Marine, was refused on the basis that another operator who had sustained heavy losses on its Irish Sea services could then similarly seek a subvention.

Consequently, faced with huge losses on off-peak services, Irish Ferries ceased sailings on the French routes from the end of October 1996.

The *Saint Patrick II*, which completed her last inbound sailing from Roscoff on 8th September, sailed for lay-up at Le Havre. She was demise chartered for more than four years by Hellenic Mediterranean Lines and renamed *Egnatia II* for service between Patras and Brindisi.

In 2000 she was renamed *Ville de Sète* for a service operated by Balear Express between the French port of Sète and Palma in Majorca. This proved to be short-lived and she was further sub-chartered by Hellenic Mediterranean Lines to Briar Star Ltd, operators of Swansea-Cork Ferries. Renamed *City of Cork* she returned to Irish waters in March 2001 to operate between the Welsh and Irish ports. But immediately prior to commencing service she was refused a

Killian II. The season ended with the arrival of the ship at Rosslare, from Roscoff, on 27th September, and a subsequent sailing to Le Havre for lay-up.

A year later she was sold to Cape Enterprise Ltd, Panama, who renamed her *Medina Star*. She sailed to Piraeus, Greece, where she was laid up. In 2000 she was sold again, to Green Island Maritime Ltd, and again in 2001 to the Commercial Bank of Greece, but was still in lay-up. Eventually, in 2002, she was chartered to Hellenic Mediterranean Lines and renamed *Egnatia III*. Following a refit she entered service in May 2003 on the Patras-Igoumenitsa-Korfu-Brindisi run. June 2004 saw her chartered to Algérie Ferries for its services from

The *Saint Killian II* goes astern from Rosslare harbour outward bound for Cherbourg. (Miles Cowsill)

passenger certificate by the UK Maritime Coastguard Safety Agency because her Greek/Polish engine room crew failed to pass safety drills. The service got under way on 19th March but in June was briefly suspended again for the same reasons. The ship was subsequently sold to the Canadian Government's CTMA line for cruises on the St Lawrence and was renamed *CTMA Vacancier*.

The 1997 Ireland-France service commenced with a sailing from Rosslare to Le Havre at 16.00 on 25th March. The daily sailing in both directions, which since 1982 had operated from May to September, was replaced by a sailing on alternate days with the *Saint

Bejaia, Algiers and Oran to Marseille, and from Oran to Alicante. On completion of this charter in January 2005 the *Egnatia III* was laid up at Eleusis Bay, Greece, and in September 2007 was finally sold for breaking at Alang, India.

On 18th November 1997 ICG confirmed the withdrawal of the *Saint Patrick II* and *Saint Killian II,* and the concluding of an agreement with Rederi AB for a 21-month charter of its ship the *Normandy*. This was built by Gotaverken Arendal AB in Sweden in 1982 for Sessan Linjen as the *Prinsessan Birgitta* for its Gothenburg - Frederikshavn route. Following the purchase of Sessan Linjen by Stena AB, she was chartered by Sealink UK for

The *Saint Patrick II* arrives at Pembroke Dock whilst covering on the Rosslare service. (Miles Cowsill)

its Harwich-Hook of Holland route and renamed *St Nicholas*. In January 1991 she was renamed *Stena Normandy* in readiness for the next phase of her career – opening Sealink Stena Line's new Southampton-Cherbourg route on 28th June. This service was discontinued in 1996, following which the vessel operated for Tallink between Helsinki and Tallin until the end of 1997.

The *Normandy* arrived in Dublin for refit on 17th January 1998 and emerged the following month wearing the full Irish Ferries' livery. Her first revenue-earning run was on the Rosslare-Pembroke Dock route on 29th February, covering for the *Isle of Innisfree* as she in turn relieved the *Isle of Inishmore* in Dublin.

The *Normandy* took over the Ireland-France services on 1st April 1998, on a revised sailing schedule. The services to and from Cork and Le Havre were discontinued in favour of a crossing to Cherbourg (17.5 hours, 311 nautical miles), with peak-period sailings to Roscoff (14 hours, 246 nautical miles). Ending the Le Havre and Cork services enabled Irish Ferries to maximise the use of the *Normandy* with shorter crossings, thereby maintaining a reasonable level of frequency. The winter service, discontinued in 1996, was also reintroduced.

Irish Ferries did well to turn a former Swedish ferry into a little piece of Ireland, but her overall decor defied a thorough conversion, which in any case would have made little sense on a charter of less than two years.

Nonetheless, with many popular features which included an impressive terraced show bar, aft on Deck 7, she was a leap forward from the vessels which preceded her. Thanks to an imaginative low-season fares structure she was well patronised from the start, and the *Normandy* provided a solution to Irish Ferries' need for a suitable vessel to operate its Ireland-France services. Despite her obvious age she proved very popular with increasing numbers of Continental visitors coming to Ireland (encouraged by massive publicity on the part of Bord Failte, The Irish Tourist Board) as well as with Irish tourists heading for holidays in France. Irish Ferries' own imaginative promotion of the 'cruiseferry' concept, coupled with good onboard facilities, ensured that the

The *Saint Killian II* was sold to Greek interests in 1998 and renamed *Egnatia III*. The vessel remained in the Mediterranean until 2007 when she was sold for scrap. (Richard Seville)

Normandy made a significant contribution to the company's revenue.

In November 1999, when Rederi AB Gotland put the *Normandy* up for sale, it came as no real surprise when ICG purchased her for US$18.4 million (IR£13.4 million). Irish Ferries was under no illusions about her service speed and the fact that her passenger accommodation was not up to the company's usual standard, and investment in a IR£4 million refit was ordered. In January 2000 the *Normandy* sailed to Cammell Laird's at Birkenhead for much-needed attention. As well as her refurbishment she was fitted with stability sponsons, increasing her breadth by 3 metres but reducing her speed by a greater degree than expected. Consequently she was frequently well behind schedule, and her tendency to roll in heavy seas increased.

In view of the downturn in tourist numbers in Ireland in 2001, ICG made a submission to the Irish Government late that year. On condition that State assistance would be forthcoming, the company committed itself to investing in new tonnage for its Ireland-France services. The assistance could be structured as part of a Public Service Obligation (PSO) subvention, as is the case with other public transport services and in other European peripheral regions. The economies of operation on Ireland-France services are complex; given the lean days of winter, it is it is difficult to justify the size of vessel demanded by summer peak traffic.

Sessan Line ordered the *Prinsessan Birgitta* for service in Scandinavia. She was later to see service with Sealink and then acquired by Irish Ferries in 1998 for the Ireland-French services. (Ferry Publications Library)

Tough decisions followed in February 2002. The life expectancy of the *Normandy* was finite and with the introduction of new tonnage by competing Brittany Ferries, the vessel's age was becoming an issue. Then there was the challenge posed by low-cost airlines and certain other sea carriers (in some cases operating with state subvention), all of which was contributing to a reduction in summer carryings. Consequently, on 20th October, ICG announced a restructuring of its Ireland-France services.

Another factor in the equation was that competition

The former *Leinster* seen in Canada as the *Madeleine* following her sale in 1997. Today she operates on the Souris-Cap-aux-Meules service. (Richard Seville)

The former *Saint Patrick II* still operates today as the *C.T.MA. Vacancier*. (Richard Seville)

from an unusual quarter arrived on the French routes in June 2002, when P&O European Ferries introduced a new 18-hour service from Dublin to Cherbourg with its new ro-pax ferry *European Ambassador*, sailing outward on summer Saturdays and arriving back in time for the start of her regular week-night sailings to Mostyn. Despite limited onboard facilities, the ship attracted a healthy level of clientele keen to sail direct from Dublin. For the following 2 years the P&O season commenced in March but in 2005 the service was terminated as P&O withdrew from the Irish ferry market.

MORE TOUGH DECISIONS

Between 1996 and 2002 Irish Ferries increased its market share in the Irish Sea by 27% for tourist cars and 32% for freight vehicles, implying that improved turnover was not merely the result of Ireland's export-orientated growth. Furthermore, in 2004, the Irish travel trade presented the company with the Best Ferry Award for the 8th year running, applauding Irish Ferries' success in consistently achieving high standards of customer service.

Despite these facts and accolades, from 2003/4 Irish Ferries' financial position began to weaken. Its RoCE (Return on Capital Employed) was in a downward trend, from 9.8% in 2002 to 7.4% in 2003, 5% in 2005 and a

predicted 1.2% in 2007. To put these figures into context, the annual rate of profitability necessary for the business to recover and renew its assets is a RoCE of 15%. The reasons for the negative trend were unprecedented adverse trading conditions, exacerbated by an 85% increase in fuel costs between 2004 and 2006. The car ferry market was in retreat generally, suffering a 10% decline from 2003-2005, casualties of which included the closure of the fledgling Irish Sea Express (150 jobs lost), the termination of P&O Ferries routes (1,200 redundancies) and the withdrawal of two SeaCat routes.

Furthermore, given the international nature of the industry, most of the company's competitors had a significant cost advantage since they employed outsourced crews. P&O, for example, operated six vessels on the Irish Sea, all registered in the Bahamas, while the ship of Swansea-Cork Ferries sailed under the flag of St Vincent and Grenadines, enabling both P&O and SCF to keep the wages bill far lower than that faced by Irish Ferries. Stena Line too admitted that the profitability of its ferry operations was minimal due to intense pricing pressure on fares and to high operating costs. And ICG forecast that if no decisions were made to steer a more stable financial course, a loss was inevitable by the end of 2007 – particularly in the face

The *Normandy* leaves Cherbourg outward bound for Rosslare. (Miles Cowsill)

of stiff competition, mainly from Ryanair, which was putting the whole business under threat. The long and the short of it was that if it was to survive, ICG had to make drastic and urgent changes, however unsavoury.

Hence the decision was made to outsource crews on the continental routes, and a redundancy package was put to the existing crews concerned. The *Normandy* was withdrawn from French service at the end of November 2004 and some 125 permanent and 25 temporary crew members took voluntary redundancy. In preparation for the 2005 season, beginning in March, the bulk of crewing responsibilities were contracted out to Dobson Fleet Management Ltd, a professional ship management agency. When the *Normandy* returned to service, she was once again registered in Nassau, flying the flag of the Bahamas.

Despite wide acceptance of the redundancy offer, including by the crew of the *Normandy*, tensions ran high. On 23rd May 2005 the situation boiled over when industrial action by Irish, French and British seamen – the vast majority of whom had not been Irish Ferries employees – prevented the *Normandy* from berthing at Cherbourg, and again at Roscoff on 10th June. The latter was ended by a court order secured in France by Irish Ferries and enforced by a sizeable contingent of the Compagnies Républicaines de Sécurité (French riot

police). In defence of outsourcing crews for the *Normandy*, Irish Ferries relied on the agreement made with the former crew members' trade unions. Nevertheless, in June 2005 the dispute was referred to an independent mediator. The matter was resolved six weeks later, albeit on a temporary basis.

On 18th July a group of 50 seamen from Brittany Ferries' *Barfleur* once again took action at Cherbourg, delaying the berthing of the *Normandy* by three hours. They scuffled with Cherbourg dockers but the arrival of the Gendarmerie ended their protest. In an astute move, Irish Ferries sought legal advice from a law firm in Paris. The advice they received was that the case could be won only if Irish Ferries was able to produce photographic evidence of the disruptions. Come the next inevitable incident, Irish Ferries duly had a photographer on hand at the port to capture the behaviour of the unruly crowds. Under French law this made the dockers and the crew of the *Barfleur* responsible for any losses incurred by Irish Ferries, and the demonstrations came to an abrupt end.

In retrospect, if ICG perhaps made any significant mistake at all on its entry into the short-sea sector through the purchase of B&I Line, it's possible to point a finger at the decision to retain, in general, the staffing levels onboard its ships. Unlike Stena Line, which

At Irish Continental Group's AGM in Dublin, 2013 – Chairman, John McGuckian and Eamonn Rothwell, Chief Executive.

completely restructured its manning arrangements throughout the fleet of its newly-acquired Sealink business in 1991, Irish Ferries had largely maintained the status quo since the B&I Line restructure of 1988. Only when a dip in profits was incurred did the commercial realities of privatisation and competition became apparent. Return on capital was predicted to reach 5%, well below the company's cost of capital of 8%, and by 2007 it was predicted to sink to just 1%. The loss of

The *Normandy* was replaced by the *Oscar Wilde* in 2007.
(FotoFlite)

duty-free alone had cost the company €10m per year.

Irish Ferries responded to these difficulties – market conditions, high fuel costs and increasing competition from rival shipping operators and low-cost airlines – with a plan to restructure the company. There was no doubting the seriousness of the situation, and strong words were used: "Time has run out for Irish Ferries. Change is needed *now* to bring the company's cost base into line with its sea competitors, to compete with low-cost airlines and to ensure a future."

Further outsourcing was seen as the only possible solution to achieving these do-or-die objectives. On 19th September 2005, with a sound business plan and foundation in place on the French routes, Irish Ferries offered generous voluntary redundancy packages to its 543 Irish Sea seafarers – 8 weeks' pay for every year of service, with no upper limit. The offer was up to four times the level of statutory packages, and over 90% accepted it. Incoming Latvian workers were equally satisfied with the prospect of earning at least €17,300 per annum – more than 4 times the average Latvian industrial wage of €3,900, and a massive step up the economic and social ladder.

For Irish Ferries the stakes were even greater: the

Irish Ferries acquired from Color Line the *Kronprins Harald* for a replacement to the *Normandy* on its Irish-French services. (Mike Louagie)

savings these measures would deliver were the lifeline which could guarantee the company's long-term viability and survival – echoes of the conclusion reached by the Irish Labour Court in its judgement of 24th February 2005 in relation to the outsourcing of crew members for the *Normandy*. "The type of arrangements proposed by the company are now commonplace within the shipping industry internationally," it said.

Although the Seamen's Union of Ireland, representing ratings, was broadly in favour of the sweeping changes introduced by Irish Ferries, the trade union which represented the ships' officers, SIPTU, came out against them. This was nothing new: for several years numerous attempts had been made, unsuccessfully, to reach agreement on such sensitive issues as outsourcing crew members, and in 2004 SIPTU had called 2 strikes. Consultants nominated by SIPTU were subsequently appointed to conduct "a thorough examination into all aspects of Irish Ferries' financial position" and to "develop a set of recommendations designed to meet the requirements of the business for consideration by both parties."

The consultants had full access to company records and came to the same conclusion reached by the

company: that by the end of 2007 Irish Ferries would be unprofitable, stating that "given the current business model, the projections are not unreasonable."

After years of failed negotiations, broken promises, strikes and threatened strikes, ICG gave democracy a chance and offered its employees a choice of 3 options: vote for amended working arrangements, accept the redundancy package, or reject both offers. Within days, and before a deadline was given, 86% of employees signed written acceptances of the redundancy package – and this figure comprised a clear majority of both SIPTU and Seamen's Union of Ireland members. By the deadline over 90% had opted for voluntary redundancy.

In an earlier dispute involving SIPTU, in December 1987, the then Minister for Finance had said there was no room for brinkmanship. "The officers will accept the overall plan or, if not, B&I Line will close from Friday." This was not the B&I that could never go bankrupt because of Government subsidies; this was the real world, where sails had to be trimmed if the ship was to survive the storm, and there was no State bail-out.

In late November 2005 the outsourcing of the crewing on the *Ulysses*, the *Jonathan Swift* and the *Isle of Inishmore* commenced. The arrival of the agency crew

The *Oscar Wilde* loads at Cherbourg for Rosslare as Brittany Ferries' *Cotentin* leaves for Poole in October 2011. (Ferry Publications Library).

led to a standoff between management and seafarers, and to an intense political debate in Ireland. On 9th December 2005 a nationwide day of protest against the company's actions was called by the Irish Council of Trade Unions. The dispute was ultimately resolved through the Irish Labour Relations Commission, but not before SIPTU conducted a long and bitter campaign seeking to force the company to reverse its outsourcing policy.

In relation to the company's French services, more decisions were facing Irish Ferries. With shipyard order books full, and the prospect of paying more than €100 million for a new vessel, there was only one realistic option to strengthen the fleet – source an existing ship. Hence in September 2007 Irish Ferries took delivery of the 1989-built *Kronprins Harald* from the Norwegian shipping company Color Line. Renamed *Oscar Wilde* she entered service in December 2007 on the Rosslare-Pembroke Dock route, and finally on her intended route – Rosslare-Cherbourg and Rosslare-Roscoff. Instead of receiving the traditional white hull of Irish Ferries she maintained the blue hull of Color Line.

At the renaming of the *Oscar Wilde* in 2008, Mrs Ann Reilly (Godmother) and Eamonn Rothwell. (Irish Ferries)

Eamonn Rothwell, Mrs Ann Reilly (Godmother), Alan Stanford (Theatre Director, Actor and Oscar Wilde historian), Captain Brian Gordon – January 2008, Dublin. (Irish Ferries)

Oscar Wilde

Top left: De-Luxe Suite on Deck 8
Left: The Berneval Restaurant
Top right: Oscar's Bar
Middle right: Gaiety Lounge
Top right: The Merrion Lounge

All photos Maritime Photographic

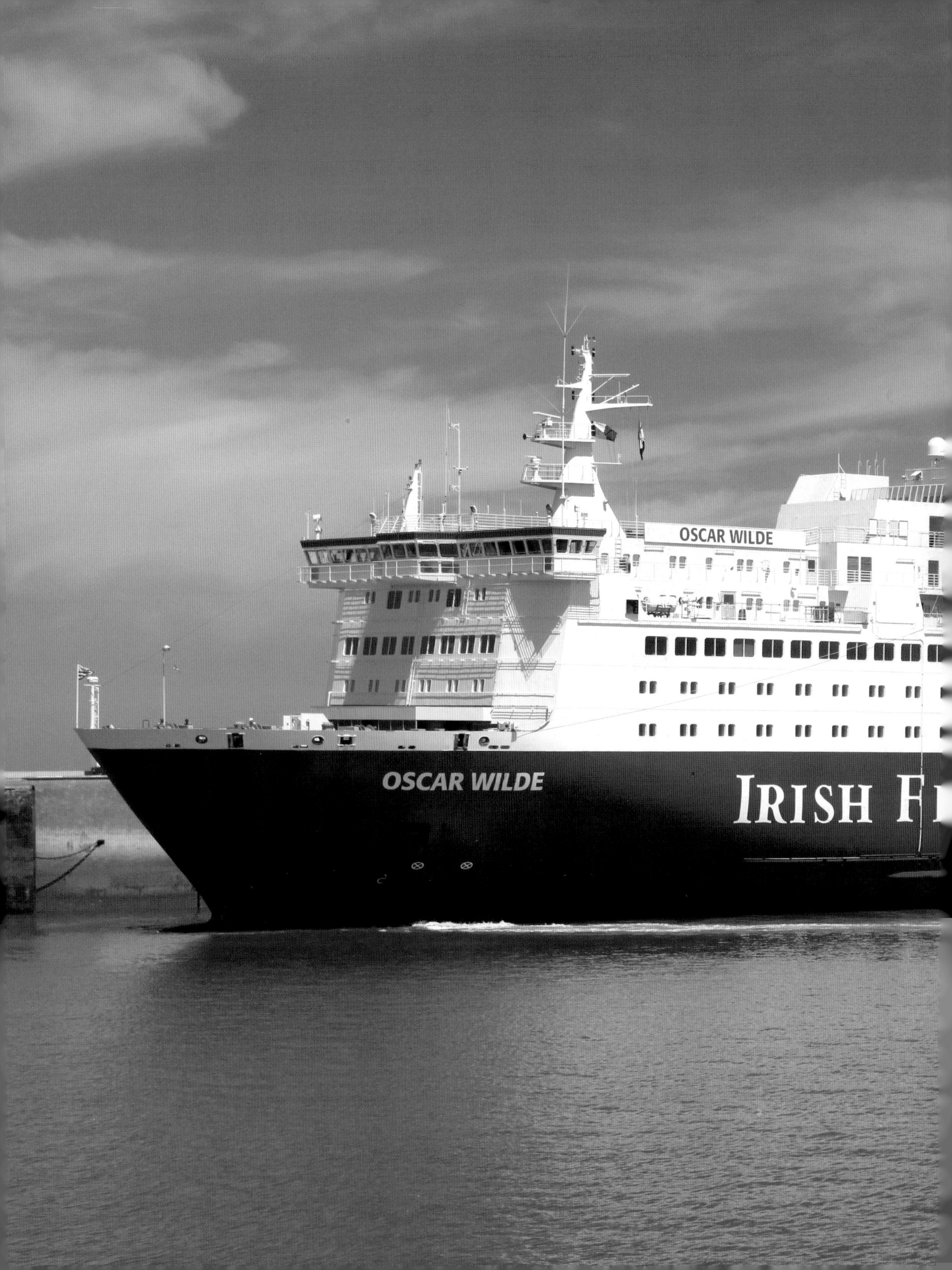
OSCAR WILDE
OSCAR WILDE
IRISH F

The *Oscar Wilde* arrives at Roscoff in May 2012 inward bound from Rosslare.
(Miles Cowsill)

OSCAR WILDE
NASSAU

Chapter ten

Onwards

By 2010 the roar of the Celtic Tiger economy had become a pitiful whimper. Elements of the Irish media were now conceding that ICG, and boss Eamonn Rothwell in particular, having endured a public flogging for the company's decision to flag-out and bring in agency crews, had been wise in preparing the ground in advance of the global economic crisis.

The Irish Independent, reporting in March 2011, said that Eamonn Rothwell had once again defied the odds, the ferry company delivering a very healthy 19% increase in profits for 2010. "The latest Irish Continental results demonstrate just how necessary the radical surgery performed by Mr Rothwell in 2005 really was. In 2004, the last full year before the company flagged out its crews, Irish Continental's staff costs amounted to almost €68m. This had fallen to just €24m by 2010, a reduction of almost €44m. While its labour costs are now much lower than they were in 2005, Irish Continental's fuel costs have risen, climbing by a further €10m to €41.4m last year. All of which means that doing nothing was not an option for Irish Continental. If it had continued as before, last year's €31.5m operating profit would have been transformed into a €12.5m loss." *(Publisher's Note : The above report does not include the cost of the outsourcing of ICG's crewing but the overall savings on wage costs between 2014 and 2010 were about 30% - source ICG).*

Such success from an indigenous Irish company, operating in a difficult sector, was all the more commendable for its rarity. And, remarkably, ICG's 2010 results also defied the fact that while passenger numbers rose by almost 8% to 1.53 million (due in no small part to the disruption to air traffic caused by the Icelandic volcanic ash cloud), the number of freight units carried was down by 9% to 178,000, and cars down by 2.4% to 367,000.

ICG ASHORE AND AFLOAT

ICG comprises two main divisions – Ferries Division and Container & Terminal Division – and within each are subsidiary companies.

Dublin Port is the Republic of Ireland's premier seaport, with a total throughput in 2011 of 28 million tonnes. ICG plays a very significant role in this success, not just through ro-ro traffic but also for lift-on/lift-off container services.

Dublin Ferryport Terminals (DFT) is part of the Container & Terminal Division of ICG and operates the most modern container terminal within the Dublin Port estate, strategically located within 3 km of Dublin City

Centre and just 1 km from the Dublin Port Tunnel, which provides direct access to Ireland's motorway network. The terminal's facilities comprise 480 metres of berths for container ships, with a depth of 9 to 11 metres and equipped with three modern Liebherr gantry cranes (40-tonne capacity), eight rubber-tyred gantries (40-tonne capacity) and a reachstacker (45-tonne capacity). DFT provides container-handling services to its sister company Eucon, as well as to third-party customers. High-frequency container freight services also operate from DFT's terminal in Dublin Port to Rotterdam, Antwerp and Radicatel, with connections to Cork and Belfast.

Any lingering notion that ICG's involvement in the Port of Belfast ended with the cessation of the Belfast Ferries operation in 1990 is mistaken; Belfast Container

Dublin, Cork and Belfast with Rotterdam, Antwerp and Rouen (Radicatel).

A former wholly-owned ICG subsidiary, sold in December 2012 for €29m, was Rotterdam-based Feederlink Shipping & Trading B.V. Since its inception in February 1993 Feederlink had become the established leader in container feeder operations, with strong roots in Scotland and England and providing high-frequency scheduled services between the deep-sea hub ports of Rotterdam and Felixstowe on one side and Immingham, Teesport, South Shields and Grangemouth on the other. This reliable service of pre-agreed feeder connections successfully satisfied the linked and inter-dependent needs of deep-sea lines, logistics providers and end users. At the same time it delivered other important benefits – not least, taking the strain off overstretched

The container vessel *Eucon Progress* en route in the English Channel. (FotoFlite)

Terminal is in fact an important part of ICG's Container & Terminal Division. Located on the County Antrim side of the port, the 11.5-acre site is equipped with a mobile crane (100-tonne capacity) and three straddle carriers.

As for the ICG ships which transport the containers and associated lift-on/lift-off equipment, these are operated very successfully by Eucon. This provides a short-sea door-to-door service between Ireland and Continental Europe, plus dedicated feeder services to the major deep-sea container ports in the UK and Europe. The modern fleet of ICG container vessels includes the largest and fastest ships in the short-sea trade, renowned for schedule reliability, and connects

road and rail networks and, in the process, reducing CO_2 emissions.

THE BUYOUT BATTLE FOR ICG

With ICG having completed an investment programme of €500 million in creating the most modern ferry fleet in western Europe, Chief Executive Officer Eamonn Rothwell next turned his attention to the needs of the Group itself.

In 2007 Aella (owned and controlled by Eamonn Rothwell and senior managers Finance Director Garry O'Dea, Marketing Director Tony Kelly, Company Secretary Thomas Corcoran and Operations Director John Reilly) made an offer for ICG in response to a request by ICG's biggest institutional shareholder for a liquidity event. Although ICG's Board recommended acceptance of the Aella offer, the offer was frustrated by the rival interest of a consortium called Moonduster (A combination of One51 and Doyle Stevedoring) which, following the Board's recommendation of acceptance of Aella's offer, each built up a stake of 12.5% in ICG. Liam Carroll's South Morston investment company then purchased a 29% stake in ICG. Aella offered €24 per share but both Moonduster and South Morston rejected it.

In November 2009, South Morston's shares were placed by Allied Irish Bank with over 30 institutions at a price of 12.20 Euro, roughly half of what was paid for the stock in 2007.

THE *PRIDE OF BILBAO*

An excellent example of ICG's ability to recognise and capitalise on a lucrative long-term profit opportunity was the shrewd IR£56 million purchase from Rederi AB of Viking Line's 37,500 tonnes luxury ferry *Olympia*, newly installed on charter to P&O European Ferries as the *Pride of Bilbao*. The purchase was facilitated thanks largely to the support of a financing arrangement agreed

The *Jonathan Swift* arrives at Holyhead on her morning sailing from Dublin. (Gordon Hislip)

with ICG banks which took only five weeks to complete.

The P&O charter was due to expire in April 1996 but with options to renew for a further 5½ years. Although ICG could not be certain that P&O would take up the option, the existing charter would generate annual revenue for ICG of IR£9 million which, after payment of 6.9% interest to the bank on the finance raised, would leave a yearly profit of IR£600,000. In the event P&O *did* take up its option and the *Pride of Bilbao* was further chartered until 1998 and subsequently extended again

At the Irish Continental Group's AGM in Dublin, 2013, the Board of Directors. Left to right: Bernard Somers, Brian O'Kelly, Tom Corcoran, John McGuckian (Chairman), Eamonn Rothwell (CEO), Garry O'Dea, Catherine Duffy, Tony Kelly. (Irish Ferries)

The *Olympia* was built for Viking Line for its service between Stockholm and Helsinki. She is seen here inward bound to Sweden during her last year in service with the company. (Viking Line)

P&O Portsmouth acquired the former *Olympia* to open its rival ferry service to Brittany Ferries to Bilbao. The former Scandinavian vessel arrives here at Portsmouth inward bound from Spain. (Ferry Publications Library)

The *Isle of Innisfree* laid up at Dublin prior to her charter to P&O Portsmouth. (Miles Cowsill)

The former *Isle of Innisfree* was renamed by P&O Portsmouth the *Pride of Cherbourg* and replaced the two 'Super Viking' vessels on the route. The former 'Innisfree' was not suitable for the Portsmouth-Cherbourg route as she lacked sufficient cabin accommodation for the service. With reorganisation of the P&O ferry operations, the Portsmouth-Cherbourg route was closed in 2005 as part of rationalisation measures with severe competition on all English Channel operations. (Miles Cowsill)

With the closure of the Portsmouth-Bilbao service by P&O Ferries in 2010, Irish Ferries renegotiated the charter of the vessel to St. Peter Line for specialist cruise excursions from St Petersburg. (Bruce Peter)

to 2002 and again beyond that – for another 5 years in fact. ICG favoured the charter arrangement rather than operating the ship as part of its own fleet because although the vessel had the capacity and facilities to cater for seasonal tourist traffic, it would have been uneconomical to operate in off-season. So maintaining the charter arrangement was a much more viable business proposition in the longer term.

However, a further charter extension to 2010 was the last; in autumn of that year P&O ceased sailings between Portsmouth and Bilbao and, on 10th December

after lay-up at Falmouth, the ship was purchased by St. Peter Line for €37.7 million. Following refit she entered service as the *SPL Princess Anastasia* on the St. Petersburg-Helsinki-Stockholm-Tallinn link.

ICG's purchase of the *Pride of Bilbao* (along with taking a 25% holding in container ship operator Bell Lines) indicated not only the financial stability of the company but also ICG's shrewd expertise in the charter business. Indeed, the company took great pride in the fact that its ship the *Saint Patrick II* had never failed to secure a charter, once tendered for.

Today the former *Isle of Innisfree* operates in New Zealand between the two principal islands of the country. Her profile as the *Kaitaki* has little changed from her days on the Irish Sea. (Darren Holdaway)

The
Fleet

ULYSSES

Built at Aker Finnyards, Rauma, this 12-deck vessel has extensive facilities, the themes and names of which were inspired by the James Joyce novel *Ulysses*. In 2001, just two months into service, the *Ulysses* won the prestigious 'Most Significant New Build: Ferry Category Award' from *Cruise & Ferry* magazine.

In her first 10 years of operation she made around 14,000 crossings, a distance of 826,000 nautical miles – equal to 33 times around the world! Bad weather conditions have never caused her to remain in port.

Although no longer the largest ferry in the world in terms of car capacity, the *Ulysses* remains the biggest operating on Irish Sea routes. At 51,000 tonnes she has capacity for up to 2,000 passengers and 1,342 cars.

Vehicle accommodation

More than 26 metres longer than her predecessor the *Isle of Inishmore*, the *Ulysses* accommodates up to 1,342 cars or 240 trucks (or any practical combination of both) on the 4,076 lane metres (2.6 miles) of vehicle decks, 4 of which are fixed and 1 (Deck 8) is hoistable. The lower trailer deck can accommodate 345 lane metres of traffic. The main trailer deck (Deck 3) has 1,402 lane metres of space. The upper trailer deck (Deck 5) has 1,341 lane metres and the top trailer deck (Deck 7) has 988 metres. Exterior curved ramps are located fore and aft on the port side, allowing cars and vans to drive between the upper and top trailer decks in order to speed loading and unloading.

Engines

The *Ulysses* is powered by 4MAK 9M 43 main engines which develop a total output of 31,200 kw (41,808 hp). They are linked in pairs to gearboxes which

Ulysses

Gross Tonnage:	50,938
Year Built:	2001
Dead-weight Tonnage:	10,722
Length Overall:	209.02 metres
Breadth:	31.84 metres
Draught :	6.40 metres
Speed:	22 knots
Capacity:	1,342 cars or 240 trucks
Passengers:	1,875

reduce the speed to 144.4 rpm and in turn, via the shafts, drive 2 5.1m-diameter LIPS type 4C16 controllable pitch propellers, attaining a vessel speed of 22 knots. The ship has 4 LIPS-type CT75 side thrusters, each of 2,400 kw and fitted with a 2.75 m-diameter propeller. She has two Becker FKSR flap rudders, with a surface of 16.4 square metres, giving a 65-degree angle of turn on each side.

James Joyce Balcony Lounge - *Ulysses* (Maritime Photographic)

Café Lafayette - *Ulysses* (Maritime Photographic)

Isle of Inishmore

Gross Tonnage:	34,031
Year Built:	1997
Dead-weight Tonnage:	5,192
Length Overall:	182.5 metres
Breadth:	27.8 metres
Draught	6.0 metres
Speed:	21 knots
Capacity:	856
Passengers:	2,330

Oscar Wilde

Gross Tonnage:	31,914
Year Built:	1987
Dead-weight Tonnage:	5,250
Length Overall:	166.26 metres.
Breadth :	28.40 metres.
Draught:	6.50 metres.
Speed:	21.5 knots.
Capacity:	580.
Passengers:	1,458

ISLE OF INISHMORE

She was built in Holland in 1997 for Dublin-Holyhead service as a larger replacement for the *Isle of Innisfree*. On the arrival of the *Ulysses* she was transferred to the Rosslare-Pembroke Dock route.

Engines

The *Isle of Inishmore* is powered by four Sulzer 8ZAL40S main engines which develop a total output of 24,000 kw. They are linked in pairs to gearboxes and in turn, via the shafts, drive two 4.8m-diameter LIPS-type controllable pitch propellers to achieve a speed of 21.5 knots. Fuel consumption is approximately 2.5 tonnes per hour at 19 knots. The ship has two LIPS controllable pitch bow thrusters, each of 2,400 KW, and 2 Becker flap rudders, with GSK linked Super Y, giving a 65-degree angle of turn on each side. Two Fincantieri fin stabilizers are also fitted.

OSCAR WILDE

She was built as the *Kronprins Harald* at Wartsila Turku Shipyard in Finland to operate Jahre Line's Norway/Germany link. Following the takeover of Jahre Line by Color Line, she remained on the Oslo-Kiel service until 2007, when she was sold to Irish Continental Group. On completion of her Color Line service at Oslo she was taken over by an Irish Ferries crew and sailed for dry-dock at Fredericia Skibsvaerft A/S

in Denmark for an extensive refit. This included installation of a second bow thrust unit to improve manoeuvrability in port, plus new smoke alarm systems and a full sprinkler system overhaul.

Work on the passenger areas included the construction of two new 55-seat state-of-the-art cinemas; the restyling of restaurants, bistros, lounge bars, children's play areas and other passenger facilities to reflect the *Oscar Wilde* theme; a major upgrade of the cafeteria – the Left Bank Brasserie; a new hair & beauty salon; revamping the main reception area; adding 130 new reclining seats; fitting new passenger information signs; and rebranding the ship in Irish Ferries livery.

Deck by deck

Deck 7 is the main passenger deck. Forward is the Merrion Lounge and aft is the larger Gaiety Lounge, both with entertainment facilities. The starboard side features a wide and imposing passageway, with seating and tables along the vessel's side. Off this walkway are the waiter-service Berneval restaurant, the Steakhouse, the Café Lafayette, Oscar's Piano Bar, a games zone and a children's play area. There is a central staircase towards the bow, and on the port side is the tastefully-appointed Left Bank caféteria.

On **Deck 5** is the information desk and themed foyer, off which are the shop and the hair and beauty

Jonathan Swift

Gross Tonnage:	5,989
Year Built:	1999
Dead-weight Tonnage:	455
Length Overall:	86.6 metres
Breadth:	24.0 metres
Draught:	3.2 metres
Speed:	39 knots
Car Capacity:	200
Passengers:	798

Kaitaki

Gross Tonnage:	22,365
Year Built:	1995
Dead-weight Tonnage:	5,794
Length Overall:	181.60 metres
Breadth:	23.40 metres
Draught:	5.60 metres
Speed:	21.5 knots
Capacity:	600
Passengers:	1,760

salon. Cabin accommodation, from 2 to 5-star and all en suite, is on **Decks 5 to 9** inclusive, and suites offer an additional choice. On **Deck 10** are reserved seat lounges and two cinemas.

The bridge is on **Deck 9**. **Decks 3** and **4** are vehicle decks, an internal ramp accessing the upper deck.

JONATHAN SWIFT

She was built for Irish Ferries in 1999 by Austal Ships of Australia. The twin-hulled aluminium 86-metre fastcraft is capable of maintaining 39 knots between Dublin and Holyhead. She offers panoramic views, a Club Class lounge, bar, café and a brasserie. The *Jonathan Swift* travels over 162,000 Kms a year.

KAITAKI (ex-ISLE OF INNISFREE)

Built for Irish Ferries in 1995 for the Dublin-Holyhead link, she operated the Rosslare-Pembroke Dock service on arrival of the *Isle of Inishmore*. In 2001 she was displaced by the *Isle of Inishmore* on the Rosslare route and offered for charter or sale. She remains in the ownership of ICG and since 2002 has been chartered to P&O Portsmouth Ltd and subsequently sub-chartered by P&O Ferries to Stena Line, serving in Swedish waters as the *Stena Challenger*. In 2005 a further sub-charter took her to Interislander (a division of the New Zealand rail company, KiwiRail) to serve on the Cook Strait route between Wellington and Picton. The charter has been renewed again directly with ICG by Interislander for a further four years from July 2013.

Reception Area - *Isle of Inishmore* **(Maritime Photographic)**

Deck 7 Entrance to Club Class Lounge - *Isle of Inishmore* **(Maritime Photographic)**

Irish Ferries/B&I Line- Fleet List 1965 - 2013

Name	Built	Tonnage	Passengers	Cars	Operator	Notes
Bison	1975	14,426	76	Ro-Ro	B&I Line	Ro-Ro
Connacht	1979	6,800 gross	1,500	332	B&I Line	
Cu na Mara	1980	267 gross	267	0	B&I Line	Boeing Jetfoil
Dragon	1967	6,141	850	250	Normandy Ferries	
Dundalk	1939	—	—	Cargo	B&I Line	
Dundalk	1975	2,353 gross	12	350	B&I Line	Ro-Ro
Earl Harold	1971	5,509 gross	1,800	190	B&I Line	Chartered from Sealink British Ferries
Fennia	1966	6,178 gross	1,200	255	B&I Line	Chartered from Silja Line
Glanmire	1936	—	—	—	B&I Line	Cargo
Inniscara	1938	—	—	—	B&I Line	Cargo
Innisfallen (III)	1948	3,706 gross	472	0	B&I Line	
Innisfallen (IV)	1969	4,848 gross	1,149	280	B&I Line	
Innisfallen (V)	1969	4,849 gross	1,380	280	B&I Line	Ex-Leinster (VI)
Isle of Inishmore (I)	1981	6,807 gross	1,500	386	Irish Ferries	
Isle of Inishmore (II)	1997	34,031 gross	2,200	856	Irish Ferries	
Isle of Inishturk	1981	6,807 gross	1,500	386	Irish Ferries	Ex-Isle of Inishmore (I), ex-Leinster (VI)
Isle of Innisfree (I)	1986	11,763 gross	2,000	411	B&I Line/Irish Ferries	Chartered from Stena RoRo
Isle of Innisfree (II)	1995	22,365 gross	1,650	600	Irish Ferries	Chartered to KiwiRail, Interislander, NZ
Jonathan Swift	1999	5,992 gross	600	160	Irish Ferries	High speed craft
Juniper	1977	5,610 gross	12	Ro-Ro	Irish Ferries	Chartered
Kildare	1970	—	0	Cargo	B&I Line	
Kilkenny	1937	—	0	Cargo	B&I Line	
Kilkenny	1973	3,644 gross	0	Cargo	B&I Line	Lift-on/Lift-off
Lady of Mann	1976	3,083 gross	800	130	B&I Line	Chartered from IoM Steam Packet
Leinster (IV)	1948	4,753 gross	1500	0	B&I Line	
Leinster (V)	1969	4,849 gross	1380	280	B&I Line	Renamed Innisfallen (V)
Leinster (VI)	1981	6,807 gross	1500	386	B&I Line	Renamed Isle of Inishmore (I)
Leopard	1968	6,113 gross	850	250	Normandy Ferries	
Meath	1960	2,475 gross	0	Cargo	B&I Line	
Munster (IV)	1947	4,115 gross	1500	0	B&I Line	
Munster (V)	1968	4,007 gross	1000	220	B&I Line	
Munster (VI)	1970	7,993 gross	1040	238	B&I Line	
Normandy	1981	17043 gross	2100	700	Irish Ferries	
Norröna	1973	7,457 gross	1040	250	B&I Line	Chartered from Smyril Line
Oscar Wilde	1987	31,914 gross	1438	550	Irish Ferries	
Pride of Bilbao	1986	37,583 gross	2553	600	Irish Ferries	Chartered to P&O European Ferries
Prinsessan Desiree	1971	5,694 gross	1400	250	B&I Line	Chartered from Sessan Line
Prins Hamlet	1973	5,829 gross	1100	275	B&I Line	Chartered from DFDS Seaways
Prins Philippe	1973	5,643 gross	1302	243	B&I Line	Chartered from RMT
Purbeck	1978	2,736 gross	58	Ro-Ro	Irish Ferries	Chartered from Truckline

Saint Killian II (FotoFlite)

Top: : The *Leinster*, with her shortlived blue funnel, rests in Princes Dock with sister Munster. (Ian Collard)

Left: Entering the lock stern first, the *Munster* arrives in Liverpool from Dublin.(Ian Collard)

Above: The *Leinster* pulls away from Brocklebank Dock before coming to starboard and passing into the Mersey through Langton Lock. (Ian Collard)

Name	Built	Tonnage	Passengers	Cars	Operator	Notes
Saint Colum I	1973	7,819 gross	1090	230	Belfast Car Ferries	Ex-Saint Patrick
Saint Killian	1973	7,125 gross	1500	320	Irish Continental Line	
Saint Killian II	1973	10,256 gross	2000	418	Irish Continental Line	Ex-Saint Killian
Saint Patrick	1973	7,819 gross	1090	230	Irish Continental Line	To Belfast Car Ferries 1982
Saint Patrick II	1973	7,984 gross	1500	420	Irish Ferries	
Senlac	1973	5,550 gross	1400	217	B&I Line	Chartered from SNCF
Stena Germanica	1967	3,658 gross	1300	220	B&I Line	Chartered from Stena Line
Stena Nordica (II)	1975	5,443 gross	1200	450	B&I Line	Chartered from Stena Line
The Viking	1974	4,655 gross	1200	330	B&I Line	Chartered from Sally Line
Tipperary	1979	14,087 gross	12	Ro-Ro	B&I Line	Chartered from P&O
Ulysses	2001	50,938 gross	1875	1342	Irish Ferries	
Viking III	1964	3,824 gross	940	180	B&I Line	Chartered from Townsend Thoresen
Wicklow	1938	—	0	Cargo	B&I Line	Cargo
Wicklow	1971	3,664 gross	0	Cargo	B&I Line	Lift-on/Lift-off

Departure of the Dublin Boat! The *Leinster* leaves Liverpool's Princes Dock behind as she makes her way through the system to lock out into the Mersey for another Irish Sea crossing. High above on the flying bridge the Master, joined by the Chief Officer, is seen peering over the side as he skilfully manoeuvres his command through the confines of the dock. In the distance, the Victoria Clock Tower marks the lock where he will put the ship alongside for the pump down to river level. (Ian Collard.)

Index

Illustrations are highlighted in **bold**